IDIOTS
AT WORK

Other Books by Leland Gregory

What's the Number for 911?
What's the Number for 911 Again?
The Stupid Crook Book
Hey, Idiot!

IDIOTS
AT WORK

CHRONICLES OF
WORKPLACE STUPIDITY

Leland Gregory

**Andrews McMeel
Publishing**

Kansas City

IDIOTS AT WORK

Copyright © 2004 by Leland Gregory. All rights reserved. Printed in the United States of America. No part of this book may be used or reproduced in any manner whatsoever without written permission except in the case of reprints in the context of reviews. For information, write Andrews McMeel Publishing, LLC, an Andrews McMeel Universal company, 4520 Main Street, Kansas City, Missouri 64111.

06 07 08 RR2 10 9 8 7 6 5

ISBN-13: 978-0-7407-4699-4
ISBN-10: 0-7407-4699-5

Library of Congress Catalog Control Number: 2004102693

Book design by Holly Camerlinck
Book composition by Steve Brooker

Attention: Schools and Businesses

Andrews McMeel books are available at quantity discounts with bulk purchase for educational, business, or sales promotional use. For information, please write to: Special Sales Department, Andrews McMeel Publishing, LLC, 4520 Main Street, Kansas City, Missouri 64111.

This book is dedicated to my wife,
Gloria Gregory. Only one year
after we met you helped give me
the courage to follow my dreams
and become a self-employed writer.
It hasn't always been easy but it
sure has been a great adventure with you!

ACKNOWLEDGMENTS

I would personally like to thank the following people for helping me gather stories or for contributing their own personal anecdote (in some cases names, dates, and company names were changed to protect the idiots). Thanks a lot, guys!

Greta Beach
Jim Brockman
Donna Davis
Yvonne Ferguson
Mike Flaherty
Marguerite Glentz
Michael G. Hodowanitz
Teresa Luke
Alex Redditt
John Rozakis
J. Alec West
Fred Wilson

RSVP-RIP

The Sony Corporation decided to honor famous ragtime pianist Eubie Blake with its first Legendary Innovator Award. The company touted that Mr. Blake's attendance at the ceremony would be a tremendously "uplifting experience." Mr. Blake, however, did not attend the ceremony as he had died eight years before receiving the invitation. I guess if he did show up that would have been a tremendously "uplifting experience."

What good is the moon if you can't buy it or sell it?

—IVAN BOESKY,
Wall Street trader, eventually convicted of insider trading

A WEIGHTY SUBJECT

A woman called a travel agent and asked, "Do airlines put your physical description on your bag so they know whose luggage belongs to who?" The agent replied, "No, why do you ask?" The timid-sounding woman said, "Well, when I checked in with the airline, they put a tag on my luggage that said FAT, and I'm overweight. Is there any connection?"

After putting the woman on hold for a minute while she regained her composure, the agent explained to the woman the city code for Fresno is FAT and the airline was just putting a destination tag on her luggage. Makes you wonder if the woman saw the word "terminal" on her luggage, would she have thought she was really sick?

PUT A LID ON IT

The Gerber Company wanted to broaden its
market and began exporting its baby food
to Africa. Unlike some products and slogans
that don't quite make the translation,
everything about this product remained the
same including the trademarked adorable
little baby on the label. So was baby food
a huge success in Africa? Unfortunately,
no. You see, a large portion of the African
population can't read, so local companies
routinely put pictures of what's inside the
package on the label. Makes you wonder where
they get baby oil from, doesn't it?

We've got to pause and ask ourselves: How much clean air do we need?

—LEE IACOCCA

defending his company's resistance to tougher auto emission standards

THAT BABY WAS REALLY SMOKIN'

Charles Harper, the chairman of the R. J. Reynolds Company, was asked about the serious risks of secondhand smoke and its effect on children. The tobacco company chairman responded smugly that children do not like smoky rooms, and therefore they leave them. Someone asked about infants who don't have the ability to leave on their own. Harper cocked his head to one side and responded: "At some point, they will learn to crawl." His comment caused outrage and exposed R. J. Reynolds's butt to the public.

CUSTOMERS, CAN'T LIVE WITH THEM, CAN'T LIVE WITHOUT THEM

A customer flagged a waiter at a popular sports bar that specializes in stocking a large assortment of beers.

Customer: "Do you serve nonalcoholic beer?"

Waiter: "No, sir, I'm sorry we don't."

Customer: "Oh well, in that case just give me an O'Douls."

(Editor's note: An O'Douls is a nonalcoholic beer.)

The owner of a small-town grocery store was confused when a tourist stopped his car in the parking lot, stuck his head inside the door, and asked: "Do you know where I might find a grocery store in this town?"

A woman called a Wal-Mart store before the Christmas holidays and wanted to know the answer to this question: "How long is a nine-foot [artificial] Christmas Tree box?" Not such a strange question since the tree comes in several pieces. But then she added, "Because I need to know if I need to bring one car or two."

URINE TROUBLE NOW

The Gainers meatpacking plant in Edmonton, Alberta, Canada, is having a—well, a pissing contest with the local union. The union can't hold its temper or its water over a ruling that workers have to pay for their bathroom breaks. The Alberta arbitration board has upheld the Gainers regulation that docks the pay of workers who go to the bathroom when not on their scheduled breaks. The reasoning behind the board's decision was that refusing to pay employees who are not actually on the job (but in the bathroom or on the phone) doesn't violate the collective agreement between the union and the plant.

Representatives of Gainers stated that the policy was put in place because workers were abusing bathroom breaks (either that or they're all incontinent). The union, needless to say, is pissed off at the arbitration board's decision.

𝕴'll tell you, it's Big Business. If there is one word to describe Atlantic City, it's Big Business. Or two words—Big Business.

—Real estate tycoon **DONALD TRUMP,** quoted in a 1989 *Time* magazine

THE MOUSE THAT ROARED

The following memo to IBM field engineers is an actual warning that was distributed to all IBM branch offices.

ABSTRACT: MOUSE BALLS AVAILABLE AS
FRU (FIELD REPLACEMENT UNIT)

Mouse balls are now available as FRU. Therefore, if a mouse fails to operate or should it perform erratically, it may need a ball replacement. Because of the delicate nature of this procedure, replacement of mouse balls should only be attempted by properly trained personnel.

Before proceeding, determine the type of mouse balls by examining the underside of the mouse. Domestic balls will be larger and harder than foreign balls. Ball removal procedures differ depending upon manufacturer of the mouse. Foreign balls can be replaced using the pop-off method. Domestic balls are replaced using the twist-off method. Mouse balls are not usually static sensitive. However, excessive handling can result in sudden discharge. Upon completion of ball replacement, the mouse may be used immediately.

It is recommended that each replacer have a pair of spare balls for maintaining optimum customer satisfaction, and that any customer missing his balls should suspect local personnel of removing these necessary items.

To reorder, specify one of the following:
P/N 33F8462—Domestic Mouse Balls
P/N 33F8461—Foreign Mouse Balls

NICE WORK IF YOU CAN GET IT

We all know that CEOs and presidents of companies make a lot more money than any of their workers. But, hey, they're the bosses. It's their job to make sure the company is run correctly and everything stays afloat--they earn their money, right? Not always. Case in point: Gilbert Amelio was fired as head of Apple Computers after he helped push the company farther and farther away from recovery. Although he was in the top position for only seventeen months and did a horrible job of it, he left with a compensation package of an estimated $13.5 million. Or, how about John R. Walter? AT&T fired Walter after only nine months of management training for the huge telecommunications firm's top position. He was fired because he lacked "intellectual leadership." So what did he leave with other than his walking papers? That would be a $26 million severance package. Now let me get this straight--it's Walter who lacks intellectual leadership?

SHAREHOLDING YOUR LIQUOR

Young and Company Brewery of England announced it would discontinue serving beer, food, and wine at its annual shareholders meeting. It was discovered by some wise drinkers that the purchase of only one share of the company's stock, which sells for about $8.00, would allow them to attend the meeting and eat and drink as much as they wanted. Recently, the meetings, with hundreds of people in attendance, had broken into raucous parties. Chairman John Young announced that from now on the meetings would be limited to company business. Not only did the hundreds of one-share shareholders protest but so did an advocacy group—the Campaign for Real Ale. It called Young and Company's decision "disastrous." I'm sure that after the decision, the company's stock lost its fizz.

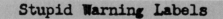

Stupid Warning Labels

**Found on a package of Sainsbury's Peanuts:
Warning: contains nuts.**

THANKS FOR NOTHING

In order to help its employees celebrate Thanksgiving and show how dearly it holds the holiday spirit, Tower Automotive of Traverse City, Michigan, gave each employee a $15 Thanksgiving grocery gift card—and then withheld $5.51 for federal and state income tax. Who's the real turkey in this situation?

If we didn't have bonuses, we wouldn't have had anybody working for us.

—A spokesperson for **DREXEL BURNHAM LAMBERT,**
explaining why the company gave over $195 million in bonuses
shortly before filing for bankruptcy

A LOOSE SCREW

A man working as a "New and Used Car Service Manager" for an automotive dealership had recently hired a new guy right out of automotive technical school. One day, the young man was having trouble loosening a stubborn bolt, and try as he might, he couldn't get the bolt to "crack." He went to the supervisor and asked for his help. The supervisor suggested that the young man heat the bolt, which is an old trick that expands the metal and makes removing the bolt easier. The technician brought out the torch, and after a few minutes, the supervisor decided to check on the young man. He'd had the flame on the bolt for several minutes, and it was now glowing a cherry red color. After a few more minutes, it began to glow a bright reddish-orange, and then the technician turned off the torch. He reached into his front pocket and pulled out a wrench, placed the circular end around the glowing bolt head, and tried to turn it off. After struggling for a few moments, he finally succeeded, and the bolt began to turn. With several turns of the wrench, the bolt was finally loose enough; he took out a folded mechanics rag to catch the bolt and placed it in his metal toolbox. At the same time, he placed the wrench in his front right pants pocket.

About two seconds later, he let out a blood-curdling scream. Everyone in the shop watched as the young man yanked the hot wrench out of his pocket and danced around the garage holding his burned leg and mumbling obscenities. The boy had gone to technical school where he should have learned one important rule of physics—steel is an excellent conductor of heat.

CHARITY BEGINS AT HOME

John Bennett, Jr., the president of a charitable foundation in Pennsylvania, was accused by the Securities and Exchange Commission of embezzling nearly $4 million in foundation money. A few months later, the foundation was forced to file for bankruptcy. Shortly afterward, Bennett protested a judge's ruling that limited him to $5,000 a month for living expenses—paid from the foundation's fund. The money was to be paid to Bennett during the duration of the proceedings, but he claimed he needed almost twice the offered amount. Let's see, he embezzled $4 million from the foundation, forced it into bankruptcy, and now he wants living expenses? If he really needs living expenses they should give him free room and board for ten to fifteen years.

THERE'S A ROACH IN MY CHICKEN

A man placed his order at a KFC in Mill Valley, California, and drove up to the window. He then requested extra biscuits and was shocked when he got two bags of marijuana instead. The stunned customer gave the bags back to the employee, drove off, and called the police. The police arrested the twenty-six-year-old worker at the restaurant. I guess the guy's brain was already extra-crispy.

Stupid Warning Labels

Found on a chain saw:
Do not attempt to stop chain with your hands.

A REAL BUTT OF A COMPANY

The huge tobacco company Philip Morris ran newspaper ads during the summer of 1995 promising to crack down on retailers who sold cigarettes to minors. In October of that year, the Minnesota state attorney general sent Philip Morris a list of retailers in the state that were known to illegally sell cigarettes to children. Philip Morris declined to do anything about it. Philip Morris Vice President Ellen Merlo said the company still intended to crack down, but "we didn't say starting today." A pack of cigarettes, a pack of lies, what's the difference?

Y2 OR NOT Y2

The highly anticipated and much dreaded Y2K bug, which actually caused fewer problems than a ladybug, brought a flurry of memos preparing employees for the worst. Here is an example of a directive sent from a company's head office in Florida, December 1999.

To: Store Manager, Photo Lab Manager, Pharmacy Manager

While we are confident in our preparations regarding the possibility of complications due to the Y2K issue, we are advising that stores in cold-weather climates order extra space heaters for the upcoming order period. This will ensure, should the power fail, that our customers will be comfortable while shopping with us.

LELAND GREGORY

JUST LET ME ASK YOU A FEW QUESTIONS FIRST

Businesses are only as good as the people they hire. We've all come across people in stores, on the phone, or in offices and wondered to ourselves "How did they get hired?" Well, sometimes there's not a lot out there to choose from. A questionnaire was sent out to vice presidents and personnel directors of the one hundred largest American corporations asking them to describe their most unusual experience interviewing prospective employees. Here are some of the responses:

- A job applicant challenged the interviewer to arm wrestle.

- Interviewee wore a Walkman, explaining that she could listen to the interviewer and the music at the same time.

- Candidate announced she hadn't had lunch and proceeded to eat a hamburger and French fries in the interviewer's office.

- Candidate said he never finished high school because he was kidnapped and kept in a closet in Mexico.

- Applicant interrupted interview to phone her therapist for advice on how to answer specific interview questions.

16

LET'S SEE WHAT DEVELOPS

A female employee of Eastman Kodak is
suing the company under the Americans with
Disabilities Act. The woman claims she
suffers from "seasonal affective disorder,"
a form of depression, and wants Kodak to
provide more light where she works--in a
photographic darkroom.

Avoid saying "hello." This elsewhere pleasant and familiar greeting is out of place in the world of business.

—Instructions of **MORGAN GUARANTY TRUST COMPANY**
to its New York employees

BIG BAD BOSS

An organization called 9to5 has an annual bad-boss contest each year. Recent runners-up for the competition were a company president who ordered his administrative assistant to substitute her urine for his for his annual drug test; and a restaurant manager who asked a waitress to wax the hair on his back. So, if these were the runners-up, who were the winners? How about a marketing manager who demanded that his administrative assistant assemble a sex toy for him? Or an assistant who had to take her boss's dog, Mitzi, to the vet and have her put to sleep? Makes that loser you work for seem a little more bearable, doesn't it? Or, does it?

RÉSUMÉ OR RÉSUMÉ NOT

In keeping with the "How did they get hired?" question posed earlier, *Fortune* magazine (July 21, 1997) put out an article that listed items from real résumés and cover letters. Here are some highlights:

- "I have lurnt Word Perfect 6.0 computor and spreadsheet progroms."

- "Wholly responsible for two (2) failed financial institutions."

- "It's best for employers that I not work with people."

- "Let's meet, so you can 'ooh' and 'aah' over my experience."

- "I have an excellent track record, although I am not a horse."

- "My goal is to be a meteorologist. But since I possess no training in meteorology, I suppose I should try stock brokerage."

- "The company made me a scapegoat, just like my three previous employers."

- "References: none. I've left a path of destruction behind me."

HEAD SHRINKER

William Aromony, the founder of the United Way of America, was on trial for diverting contributions to support his lavish lifestyle. Aromony told the court his filtering of money to use on luxury condos, multiple mistresses, and outlandish vacations was devoid of criminal intent because his judgment had been impaired due to "brain atrophy." Aromony's lawyer conceded this because it's a scientific fact that all human brains atrophy, or shrink, over time. Well, at least Aromony admitted what we all know about most bosses--they're small-minded.

Stupid Warning Labels

Found on a package of
Marks & Spencer Bread Pudding:
Product will be hot after heating.

TAKING CANDY FROM A BABY

The producers of the movie *ET* had scripted their lovable little alien to eat tiny bite-sized candy, so they immediately approached M&M's to be that candy. They went to the Mars Candy Company in New Jersey and started negotiations to use the famous candy "that melts in your mouth, not in your hands." Executives at Mars thought about the proposal, but decided they didn't want their product associated with an alien creature even if it showed the movie's audience that everyone in the universe likes M&M's. The only other bite-size candy on the market at that time was Reese's Pieces—tiny morsels of chocolate and peanut butter produced by the H. B. Reese Candy Company. Reese accepted the offer made by *ET*'s producers, not knowing exactly what they were getting into. As you know, *ET* became a megahit and one of the highest-grossing films of all times. Not only did Reese's Pieces become the favorite candy of *ET*, it also became the favorite candy of the millions and millions of children who idolized the long-fingered, big-eyed alien. After that fiasco of a decision, the egos at Mars Candy Company went to pieces.

UNCUSTOMARY CUSTOMERS

 Catalog Sales Representative: All right, sir, your order is all set up. All I need to know is what shipping method you would like. Ground is five to seven working days, we have three-day, and also overnight is available.

Customer: How long is three-day delivery?

 Computer Customer: Which side of the CD faces up when you put it in the drive?

Help Desk Representative: Shiny side goes down, label goes up.

Customer on Phone: I got this DVD last week, and it doesn't work. Can I come back and get another?

Best Buy Employee: Sure, just bring your receipt, and we will exchange it.

Customer on Phone: I stole it—I don't have a receipt. Can I still exchange it?

PHONE IT IN

The Ontario Federation of Labor in Kitchener, Ontario, Canada, installed a "bad boss" hotline to see what labor problems there were. Great idea except that soon after the number was announced, the system crashed. There were too many calls coming in for the system to handle.

It's unfair that it remain empty and unspoiled.

—**HUGH STONE,** developer of a proposed subdivision, on delays in permits to begin construction

CAST YOUR WEB IN FRONT OF YOU

In October 1995 *Fortune* magazine reported on the uncanny foresight of the megacompany Procter & Gamble. *Fortune* explained that P&G was ahead of the game in registering exclusive Internet addresses for their various products. Procter & Gamble had secured the rights to use, among others: bacteria.com, badbreath.com, dandruff.com, germs.com, pimples.com, toiletpaper.com, underarm.com, and diarrhea.com. If Amway, which was accused of starting the P&G devil scare, had anything to do with it, Procter & Gamble would also have satan.com.

CLOCKED OUT

An advertising agency in Little Rock, Arkansas, allows its employees a one-hour lunch break, and they can eat in the break room, go home, or go to a restaurant. One day, the office manager noted that the receptionist had clocked out for lunch more than two and a half hours earlier and hadn't returned to work. Concerned, she found the receptionist's home phone number, and acting on a hunch, called the woman.

Receptionist: Oh gosh, I'm sorry, I forgot I was at lunch.

Office Manager: You *forgot* you were at lunch?

Receptionist: Yeah, I was just doing some stuff around the house and forgot I was supposed to be working.

To which the office manager should have responded, "Oh, and I forgot to tell you that you're fired."

REACH OUT AND TOUCH SOMEONE

A happily married father of four filed
a protest with Nevada's Equal Rights
Commission after he was fired from his
job at Northwest Nevada Telco. His lawsuit
stirred up quite a bit of controversy
because the man had been passing himself
off as a woman on Telco's phone sex line.
He claims he was fired because of sex
discrimination. I wonder how many callers
called back asking for a refund.

NEWSPAPER AD:

Christmas sale. Handmade
gifts for the hard-to-find
person.

LOST IN TRANSLATION

The names Coca-Cola and Coke are so well known in America that they've almost become a generic term for any soft drink. But when the Coca-Cola Company first started exporting its product to China, there was no existing Chinese word for Coke. So Coca-Cola made up a name that when pronounced sounded much like Coca-Cola, "Ke-kou-ke-la." Great solution, but when the word was spoken in Chinese the name translated into "bite the wax tadpole" or "female stuffed with wax," depending on the dialect. Knowing that would make for a very bizarre ad campaign, Coke quickly changed to a set of characters that translated into "Happiness in the mouth."

Not to be outdone by Coke's translation problem of "bite the wax tadpole," Pepsi's "Come Alive with the Pepsi Generation" translated into "Pepsi brings your ancestors back from the grave," in Chinese.

QUESTIONS, QUESTIONS, QUESTIONS

We've all heard the expression "There's no such thing as a stupid question" right? Well, see for yourself. Here are some of the answers from a questionnaire sent out to a number of employers asking, "What's the strangest question you have been asked during an interview?"

- "What is it that you people do at this company?"

- "Why aren't you in a more interesting business?"

- "Will the company move my rock collection from California to Maryland?"

- "Does your company have a policy regarding concealed weapons?"

CONTROL Z

A member of Corel's technical support team received a call from a harried legal secretary with a problem. Her company had just upgraded their software from WordPerfect 8.0 to WordPerfect 10, and she had an urgent technical question. She said, "In WordPerfect 8, I would hit the tab key to get a tab. What key do I hit in WordPerfect 10?" The tech support person sat in silence wondering if he had become the victim of a prank. He tentatively answered, "The tab key?" and waited for the punch line. The response he got was not a joke. "Oh, that worked!" the woman happily replied and hung up. Seems as if the company should upgrade more than their word-processing software.

A FURRY FACSIMILE

Sleeping on the job costs companies dearly in lost man-hours, but in the case of a bus company in the United Kingdom, a quick catnap cost them a huge contract. The culprit was "Rigger," a stray cat adopted by Bodon Executive Coaches, who decided to get some shut-eye on the fax machine. While turning around three times before lying down, the cat stepped on the Send button and faxed confidential information to a rival firm. The firm's competition quickly put in a lower bid than Bodon's and won the contract. A company spokesman said they wouldn't put the cat to sleep for sleeping on the fax, but the next time it was ready for a nap, it would have its own comfortable basket--and that's the facts.

> I believe, there will be a world market for approximately five computers.
>
> —**THOMAS WATSON,** President, IBM, 1943

GETTING SCREWED-OVER AT WORK

We've all met someone who is passionate about their work, but according to research from the UK, one in five workers has experienced passionate sex while at work. The report revealed that the favorite sex spots for men include their desk or even the boss's office. Women, however, prefer the security of storerooms and coat closets. The Sexpose reported that couples who have been "hard at work" warn of some obstacles to their affections:

1. If you have sex in the coat closet make sure the door is locked.

2. If you put in some overtime in the boss's office, make sure the boss is out of the building.

3. If you like to "work" at your desk, make sure it's clear of paper clips, pins, and staple removers.

Gives the phrase "being tied to your desk" a real naughty meaning now, doesn't it?

ALUMINUM AND STEEL

A man who worked as a repairman at Kaiser Aluminum was fired after twenty-five years of service, and he sued to get his job back. He was let go after it was discovered that he had a "building" full of tools, hoses, and thousands of other items including a three-ton chain hoist that he had stolen from the company. One would think the man wouldn't have a chance to be rehired after stealing so much stuff, but a Superior Court judge had another thought. The judge ruled that the man wasn't guilty of possessing stolen goods because he was a kleptomaniac. He was allowed to go through with his lawsuit. The thief—oh, I'm sorry—the kleptomaniac—not only wants his old job back, he also wants back pay. As the saying goes, "it takes all kinds" and sometimes it just "takes a thief."

YOU CAN TAKE THAT TO THE BANK

The entire waitstaff at a small restaurant in Moultrie, Georgia, was given their W-2 forms so they could file their tax statements. One not particularly smart waitress was very excited when she received the form and asked for an early lunch break. The other employees thought she was going to run to a tax preparer, but they were surprised when she returned in a very foul mood. The waitress complained loudly to everyone that "the bank wouldn't cash my check," believing that the W-2 form was a huge end-of-the-year bonus. Even after the other employees explained what the form was, the woman still didn't have a clue.

In the "What were they thinking?" category: Jill Barad was paid $55 million after she was fired from Barbie doll maker Mattel.

A COMPANY WITHOUT A SOLE

The Reebok Company made a major faux pas when it named a whole new line of athletic shoes "Incubus." It took the company a long time to sneak a peek into a little book called a dictionary to find out the meaning of the word: a mythical demon who rapes women in their sleep. After that, the name definitely wasn't a shoe-in.

You'll never make it—four groups are out. Go back to Liverpool . . .

—**DECCA RECORDS EXECUTIVE** in 1962 to the Beatles

WARNING: READING THESE WARNINGS ARE DANGEROUS TO YOUR MENTAL HEALTH

Because of the litigious nature of our society a lot of companies have resorted to placing outrageously obvious warning labels on their products to ward off the "lunatics with lawyers." Here are some real examples of really "duh" warning labels.

On a packet of Nytol sleeping tablets—Warning: May cause drowsiness.

On the "CycleAware" helmet-mounted mirror—Remember: Objects in the mirror are actually behind you.

On a large folding cardboard sunshade for car windshields: "Please remove before driving."

On a car lock that loops around both the clutch pedal and the steering wheel—Warning—Remove lock before driving.

On a Halloween Batman costume—This cape does not give the wearer the ability to fly.

On a Rowenta iron—Warning! Never iron clothes on the body!

100 BOTTLES OF BEER ON THE WALL

A Brazilian court ordered Brahma Brewing
Company to pay damages plus a lifetime pension to their former senior brewer, Bernd
Naveke. Bernd claimed he was forced to quit
his job because he had become an alcoholic,
and it was the company's fault. Why? Because
he was a taster at the plant and he was
required to drink six to eight liters of
beer each day. Clocking in early in the
morning, Bernd chugged up to 3.1 gallons of
beer a day to make sure the quality was up
to standards. Strangely enough, after twenty
years on the job, Bernd developed a taste
for beer and canned himself at age forty.
The man's lawyer claimed that Brahma Brewing
was at fault for Bernd's drinking problem
because it failed to inform him of the risks
associated with drinking so much beer over
so long a period of time (of course, maybe
they did tell him, and he just forgot).
Bernd was able to tap the company not only
for a lifetime pension but also for $30,000.

THE SEEDS OF AN IDEA

Dedicated employees of a floundering car plant in Romania announced that they had a plan to eliminate the company's $20 million debt: Donate their sperm and give the proceeds to their employer. Well no, they wouldn't actually give their sperm to their employer, they would sell it and give their employer the proceeds. One report estimated that each employee would have to come up with four hundred donations. "[Management] told us to come up with a solution," said a union spokesperson. "Now we've found one that even the best economists never thought of." Management wanted to thank the employees by shaking everyone's hand—but thought better of it.

Stupid Warning Labels

**On a bottle of flavored milk drink:
After opening, keep upright.**

IT'S GOOD TO BE THE KING

According to an E*Trade proxy report, the 2001 compensation package of CEO Christos Cotsakos included $4.9 million in pay, $29 million in stock options, and forgiveness of a $15 million loan—all in a year when the company had lost $241 million. A spokesman for E*Trade, defending their agreement with Cotsakos, said the CEO's compensation, "reflects the success the company has had under his leadership." Eight months later, Cotsakos resigned.

FROM THE STUPID QUESTIONS FILE

An employee at a Chick-fil-A restaurant was shocked when he heard this question from a customer: "Are those Chick-fil-A sandwiches made with fish?"

Wal-Mart Employee (on phone): Thank you for calling your Wal-Mart Supercenter. How can I help you today?

Customer: How late are you open?

Wal-Mart Employee: We're open twenty-four hours, ma'am.

Customer: Okay, so what time do you close?

Customer: Can I ask you about the pet photo day on that sign?

Pet Store Worker: Of course . . . what's your question?

Customer: Do you have to bring your own pets?

GOOD VIBRATIONS

When the Harry Potter craze was in full swing, you couldn't go anywhere without seeing a tie-in to the phenomenally popular series of books and movies. Toy manufacturers saw the enormous potential of securing the merchandising rights and were soon cranking out toys, games, videos, etc. So when Mattel released the Nimbus 2000 broom as part of its line of Harry Potter toys, they weren't surprised by the toy's popularity. They were surprised about with whom the toy was popular. You see, the Nimbus 2000 isn't a typical broom that you put between your legs and pretend to fly—it's actually a broom with a vibrating handle that you put between your legs. Said one enthusiastic mother, "I'm thirty-two and enjoy riding the broom as much as my seven-year-old." Her review was posted on amazon.com along with the line, "My only complaint is, I wish the batteries didn't run out quite so quickly." Mattel stopped making the toy, not because they realized producing a vibrating toy designed to be used by prepubescent girls was a bad idea or because the buzz from the publicity was bad for business but because, according to a spokesperson, "It's just not a continued product in our line." So basically they're trying to sweep this one under the rug.

GOVERN-MENTAL

Every so often, a company will do some housecleaning and destroy old and outdated documents. However, in the world of government one can't be too careful with the documents that are destroyed. Here is an overheard conversation in a government office about the destruction of twenty-five-year-old "dead files."

Employer: Mr. Cooper, should I go ahead and destroy these files?

Supervisor: Yes, but just to be on the safe side, let's make two copies of everything to ensure they don't get lost first.

Stupid Warning Labels

Seen on a camera:
This camera only works when there is film inside.

SAY CHEESY!

Penthouse printed a series of nude photos it claimed were of tennis star Anna Kournikova, but it turned out they weren't. So the woman who posed, not Kournikova, sued the magazine for damages--I guess she felt falsely exposed. *Penthouse* agreed to destroy eighteen thousand copies of the magazine and pay the mistaken model an undisclosed sum. The photographer's defense in portraying the photos as that of the tennis star was innocent; he claimed he thought he was photographing Kournikova based on the size of the woman's nipples. Looks like this was simply a case of mixed doubles.

MAN CHOPS OFF TESTICLE IN JOB PROTEST

—**REUTERS** headline

A SHOCKING DISCOVERY

German inventor Harry Gaus accidentally discovered that the Conair Corporation had been using a safety mechanism he invented to shut off hair dryers that fall into water. Eleven years after the discovery, Gaus was awarded $46.1 million in a patent-infringement lawsuit. How did he learn of Conair's infringement? Gaus says Conair let the cat out of the bag. During a meeting to discuss a potential partnership, a VP for engineering mentioned the company was already marketing a dryer that "may infringe your patent." I bet Conair wished they had a shut-off valve for the loose-lipped VP.

... AND DECREASE THE SURPLUS POPULATION

Philip Morris tried to rally against anti-smoking measures in the Czech Republic by sponsoring an economic analysis of the "indirect positive effects" of early deaths. Yep, they tried putting a positive spin on people dying from using their product. The report emphasized savings on heath care, welfare, and housing for the elderly. After the bombshell of negative publicity, the company wheezed out a pitiful apology.

BUTTERING THEIR OWN POPCORN

Most of us have heard of movie critics like Roger Ebert, Joel Siegel, and Leonard Maltin, but what about David Manning of the *Ridgefield Press*? Never heard of him? That's strange, he has written favorable reviews for Columbia Pictures movies *Hollow Man, A Knight's Tale,* and *The Animal*. Well, don't feel stupid if you've never heard of him because he doesn't exist—there's no film reviewer named David Manning. Sony, the parent company of Columbia Pictures, admitted they created the fake critic for the sole purpose of giving "the thumbs-up" to their movies. Looks like Sony gave the general public the thumbs-up instead.

Stupid Warning Labels

On a packet of peanuts served on an internal flight in China (written in both English and Chinese): Open packet and eat contents.

READING, RITING & RITHMETIC

Connecticut Judge Socrates Mihalakos ruled that Nancy Sekor, a middle-school teacher who was fired from her job in 1993 for incompetence, had to be reinstated. His reasoning? Sekor was judged incompetent in only two of the three subjects she taught. However, Judge Mihalakos seems incompetent in the subject at hand.

IT'S IN THE BAG

A graphic designer was sitting in the break room holding an unopened bag of M&M's Crispy candy. The receptionist bounced into the room, noticed the candy, and asked what it was. "It's the new M&M's. I haven't tried them yet," said the designer. "Oh," said the receptionist. "What do they taste like?"

As of tomorrow, employees will only be able to access the building using individual security cards. Pictures will be taken next Wednesday and employees will receive their cards in two weeks. (From a memo distributed to employees at the the Microsoft Corp. in Redmond, Washington.)

WHAT A DIP!

Advertisers always try to push the envelope when it comes to their commercials—publicity equals sales. But when the Lipton Soup Company approved an ad that showed a man standing in line for communion holding a bowl of onion dip, presumably to improve the palatability of the body of Christ, it was immediately demonized. Reluctantly, Lipton withdrew the ad. I can see the slogan now: "Make the most from the host and savor the wafer—betcha can't eat just one."

WHY JOHNNY CAN'T READ

A systems administrator who has worked at a major university for fifteen years has received all kinds of stupid questions from clueless employees. One day she received a call from a woman in student counseling who complained that she couldn't get her e-mail to work. The administrator asked the woman to go into her configuration and relate what she had for a Post Office Protocol (POP) server. The woman said pop.usfra.edu. The administrator was puzzled because that was the proper POP. "It just won't work" the woman insisted. "It keeps telling me invalid server!" The administrator was at a loss, and instead of troubleshooting over the phone, she decided to come to the woman's office. Once there, she went into the configuration and immediately saw the problem. The woman had been spelling out the dots. It read: pop dot usfra dot edu. Was she really dot.stupid?

ALWAYS BE PREPARED

While Enron was going through bankruptcy it came to light that the company spent more than $200,000 to retain its box seats and luxury suite at Enron Field. The company argued that it made the payment only to fulfill a contractual obligation. On the other hand, it somehow failed to fulfill its contractual obligation for Enron's $200,000-a-year contribution to the local Boys and Girls Club. I just hope one day Kenneth Lay needs help crossing the street.

Stupid Warning Labels

Found on a packet of juggling balls—This product contains small granules under 3 millimeters: Not suitable for children under the age of fourteen years in Europe or eight years in the U.S.A.

A ROSE BY ANY OTHER NAME

In October 1998, a new e-commerce software company took the name Accompany. No big deal, right? But when you say the name of the company aloud, it sounds like "a company." This name lead to the following Abbott and Costello–type conversations;

Accompany Spokesperson: Hi, I'm calling from Accompany.

Person: Which company?

Accompany Spokesperson: Accompany.

Person: What company?

Accompany Spokesperson: Accompany.

Person: What company are you calling from?

Accompany Spokesperson: Accompany.

Person: I know it's a company, but which one is it?

They should have just called their company Third Base. Accompany decided to change its name to Mobshop in March 2000. No calls from Tony Soprano yet.

SPAM, SPAM, SPAM, LOVELY SPAM!

Imagine the surprise on the faces of the 250 employees in the Manhattan office of agency.com, an interactive consulting firm, when they opened their e-mail and found a spreadsheet with the salaries of every employee, including the company's chief, Kyle Shannon. Shannon, who by the way makes $150,000 if you didn't get the e-mail, said of the mailing, "It was a blunder, and it was painful." One of the first statements agency.com now makes when consulting with other companies is, "Now, be sure you don't e-mail out everyone's salary. It's not good for morale."

NICE WORK IF YOU CAN GET IT

Utek, a business development company, that finds, acquires, develops, and finances university-developed technology and brings it to technology companies, issued the following warning in its prospectus: "Our management has limited experience operating a business, has had no experience in managing and operating a business development company, and has little or no experience in corporate finance and corporate mergers." Hey, where do I sign up?

E-mail is not to be used to pass on information or data. It should be used only for company business.

—E-mail memo from **UNDISCLOSED COMPANY**

HOW TO WRITE ENGLISH GOOD

It's a well-known fact that English is a very difficult language to learn, but it also seems to be a difficult language to translate into other languages. Here are some samples of mistranslated English signs.

In a Tokyo hotel: *Is forbitten to steal hotel towels please. If you are not person to do such thing is please not to read notis.*

In a Yugoslavian hotel: *The flattening of underwear with pleasure is the job of the chambermaid.*

On the menu of a Swiss restaurant: *Our wines leave you nothing to hope for.*

In a Paris hotel elevator: *Please leave your values at the front desk.*

In the lobby of a Moscow hotel across from a Russian Orthodox monastery: *You are welcome to visit the cemetery where famous Russian and Soviet composers, artists, and writers are buried daily except Thursday.*

Two signs from a shop entrance on the island of Majorca: *English well talking* and *Here speeching American.*

FLY THE FRIENDLY SKIES

Anyone who has ever worked in a service industry knows that customers ask the dumbest questions. And the travel industry is no different. Here are some actual calls taken by travel agents throughout the United States.

- A client called his travel agency and wanted to get price quotes for a flight from Charlotte, North Carolina, to Hawaii. After the agent went over all the costs the customer asked, "Would it be cheaper to fly to California and then take the train to Hawaii?"

- An airline agent received a call from a woman who wanted to book a flight to Boston. When asked if she would like a window seat or an aisle seat the woman responded: "I want an aisle seat so my hair doesn't get messed up by being near the window."

SLEEPING ON THE JOB

A United Parcel Service cargo loader thought he would use his work break to catch up on sleep. So he found a nice, quiet, warm place to snooze on the plane he'd been loading and drifted off into dreamland. When he woke up, he looked out the bay window and realized that he wasn't the only thing that drifted away. The plane, bound for China, had taken off and was now flying over the Pacific Ocean. "It wasn't like he was ten minutes away and the pilot could just turn around," said Norman Black, a UPS spokesman in Atlanta. I'm sure when the man finally made it back home he was given his sleep-walking papers.

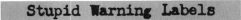

Stupid Warning Labels

Found in the instructions for a Korean kitchen knife:
Keep out of children.

COMPUTER ERROR

These days, computers are essential for handling the daily input and output of any business, even big businesses like the U.S. government. Several years back, the county controller in Reading, Pennsylvania, voiced her department's computer problem at a meeting of county commissioners. The problem was not that she didn't have a computer, it was that her computer hadn't worked in two years. She was forced to type letters, memos, and do all written business on a typewriter. "If we had a computer," she stated, "letters would go out faster." Three days after the meeting, the woman announced the computer she'd been complaining about had been fixed. The problem that had eluded her for two years? It wasn't plugged in.

PHYSICIAN, HEAL THYSELF

Consumer Reports, the advertisement-free monthly magazine that reviews products for safety and reliability, had to recall a glove compartment organizer it gave away as a free gift to new subscribers. It was discovered that the flashlight tended to overheat and cause burns, and the tire pressure gauge was inaccurate, which could cause drivers to either overinflate or underinflate their tires. The issue that followed the debacle contained an article titled "Caveat Emptor Hits Home," in which CEO Jim Guest admitted that, "We need to test any product that we offer as a premium in our own labs with the same rigor with which we rate the products you see in *Consumer Reports*." For being honest and not trying to cover up their faux pas I give *Consumer Reports* an "A" rating.

IT WOULD BE A GREAT JOB IF IT WASN'T FOR THE CUSTOMERS

Customer: Where are you located?

Shoe Store Salesperson: On MLK Boulevard.

Customer: Now, MLK Boulevard, that's on Main Street, right?

Guest Relations: It's a great day at Red Tree Country Club. This is Jack. How can I help you?

Guest: I need directions to the club.

Guest Relations: Where are you coming from?

Guest: My house.

Customer Service Rep.: When I cancel your service it is instantaneous.

Customer: Oh, so how long will that take?

STRAIGHTEN UP AND FLY RIGHT

Intense airport security is just a part of airline travel these days, and it does help to keep passengers safe or at least feeling safe. But tell that to the 1,000 passengers at the Louisville International Airport who were called back through security shortly before boarding because a screener had fallen asleep on the job. While the man was visited by the sandman, as many as 1,000 potential terrorists could have boarded national and international flights. One American Airlines flight that had already pulled away from the gate was radioed back and emptied while more than twenty other planes were delayed. Being an airline screener is one job that shouldn't be fulfilled with your eyes shut.

A LETTER SHY OF STUPID

A fabric firm was curious about why it hadn't received any mail for several days, not even junk mail. After some time, it came to light that the newly hired female letter carrier had mistaken a hole in the firm's chimney stack for the company's letter box and was dumping all their mail into the flue.

Every operating system out there is about equal. We all suck.

—Microsoft Senior Vice President **BRIAN VALENTINE** at a developers' conference describing the state of the art in operating system security.

1-800-ME-TIRED

A telephone operator in Madison, Wisconsin, sued her employer for refusing to make reasonable accommodations for her narcolepsy (a sleep disorder that can cause immediate and uncontrolled bouts of sleep). The woman was consistently late for work and had asked permission to continue arriving late because of her "disability." Isn't it great that the woman has the ability to contain her narcolepsy to the prework hours?

DON'T STRESS OUT

A government worker in Howard County, Maryland, was let go after repeatedly yelling, cursing, and making rude remarks to her supervisors. After she was fired the woman sued the state claiming her civil rights had been violated. She stated in her deposition that she suffered from manic depression, and her employer should have been required to eliminate all stressful elements from her job. Correct me if I'm wrong, but didn't they eliminate all stressful elements from her job when they fired her?

Stupid Warning Labels

Found on an ocean buoy used to determine the position of submarines: Protect from seawater.

GETTING RUBBED THE WRONG WAY

A forty-year-old left-handed telephone operator from Florida sued her employer for injuries developed on the job and was awarded $30,000 in workers' compensation. The woman, who was a phone-sex operator, had developed carpal tunnel syndrome from regularly masturbating at her station. This is a case of someone who enjoyed his or her job way too much.

We built a good company with a bad balance sheet.

—CEO **BARCLAY KNAPP,** of the telecommunications firm NTL, shortly before it filed for bankruptcy; the company's debts totaled nearly $23.4 billion

GET THE LEAD OUT

A company in Plainview, Long Island, distributed pencils to elementary schools with the slogan "Too Cool to Do Drugs" as part of an antidrug campaign. But Kodi Mosier, an observant ten-year-old, at the Ticonderoga Elementary School in New York, discovered that after the first sharpening, the message changed from "Too Cool to Do Drugs" to "Cool to Do Drugs." Next, it changed to "Do Drugs," and finally, "Drugs." A spokesperson for the company that distributed the pencils, the Bureau for At-Risk Youth, was quoted as saying, "We're actually a little embarrassed that we didn't notice that sooner." Trying to help erase their embarrassment, the company sent the boy's class a letter of apology and a box of T-shirts. No word on what the shirts said.

SO WHAT'S THE BIG STINK?

A Wisconsin judge ruled that "offensive body odor" could be considered a handicap under the state's Fair Employment Act. The law is commonly referred to as "The Pepe Le Pew Rule" (not really, I just made that up).

𝔑o one will deny that 𝔖ony is a world-class hardware company, and no one would deny that 𝔐icrosoft is a world-class software company. 𝔑intendo aspires to be neither one of those things.

—**PETER MAIN,** a Nintendo marketing executive, quoted in the *San Francisco Chronicle*

THIS JOB SUCKS!

A door-to-door salesman filed a complaint with the police in Essex (United Kingdom) stating that while he was demonstrating a vacuum at a residence, the family dog attacked him. The complaint was rejected when it came to light that the salesman was demonstrating the strength of the vacuum by trying to clean the dog. "You see, it's also a Spot remover!"

SETTING YOUR SIGHTS ON SCHOOL

Parents of children and children themselves look forward to Back to School sales—time to stock up on pencils, pens, paper, glue, scissors, and the like. But shoppers at the Wal-Mart in East York, Pennsylvania, were startled to see that the sale also included shotgun shells. A wide variety of shells were offered for that exciting first day of school from small game loads (dove shot) to skeet rounds (rollback priced to $29.80 for "a large box"). A store spokesman said the same "Back to School" price placard was used for all sale items throughout the store. So stock up for school with a full set of Stanley tools and women's intimate apparel.

WHAT RHYMES WITH BUCKET?

Drive-Thru Customer: Can I get the chicken sandwich?

KFC Employee: All of our sandwiches are chicken, sir. We have several different sandwiches to choose from.

Drive-Thru Customer: Well, I just want the one that's chicken.

KFC Employee: All of our sandwiches are chicken.

Drive-Thru Customer: Don't you have a fish sandwich?

KFC Employee: No, no, we don't have any fish, sir. Just chicken.

THEY COULD HAVE SPELLED PARE, REAP, OR PEAR . . .

A formal apology was issued by the Caldor department store chain, in Norwalk, Connecticut, after 11 million copies of an advertisement circular went out with, hopefully, a glaring error. The advertisement showed two smiling boys playing a game of Scrabble and on the board, along with several other tiled words, was the word "RAPE." Caldor claimed it had no idea who set up the board in that manner or how it got past the proofreaders. This mistake will obviously spell trouble for someone.

SNOW WHAT?

The night auditor at a local motel braved seven inches of accumulated snow and arrived at 11 P.M. to start his shift. He waved at the night clerk through the lobby windows, entered the motel, shook the snow from his coat, stamped his feet clean, and rubbed his freezing hands together to warm them up. The desk clerk, who was about to get off for the night and wasn't the brightest bulb in the chandelier, asked in all seriousness, "What's the weather like outside?" Apparently cold enough to cause brain-freeze.

There will always be crybaby boobies who are unhappy with any company.

—From a news.com interview with **MARTHA SESSUMS,** spokeswoman for DSL provider Covad, exhibiting the customer-service strategy that helped her company plummet into bankruptcy

DOWN BUT NOT OUT

The New Hampshire Supreme Court ruled that a state employee was entitled to workers' compensation payments for "work-related" depression. They made this decision even though they knew the depression the woman suffered was brought upon by the fact that she had gotten bad performance reviews.

LONG-TERM DEBT

An executive from the First National Bank of Keystone, West Virginia, pleaded guilty to embezzlement and money-laundering charges that ultimately led to the bank's failure. The man was sentenced to twelve years in prison and ordered to pay $515 million in restitution. A fair sentencing, right? Well, the catch is he has to pay back all the money he stole at the rate of $300 per month. Assuming there's no interest tagged on, he'll have the whole thing paid in full in a little over 143,000 years. Seems like the town must be home to not only the Keystone Kops but also the Keystone judges.

Stupid Warning Labels

Found on a can of insect spray: Kills all kinds of insects! Warning: This spray is harmful to bees.

LELAND GREGORY

PLEASE HANG UP AND TRY AGAIN

When all the office phones went dead, an
employee contacted the telephone repair
department of his local phone company. The
repairperson said they would be able to
service the phones the next day and would
be there between 8 A.M. and 7 P.M. The
employee asked if the repairperson could
give him a smaller time window and the
operator replied, "Would you like us to
call you before we come?" The employee
reminded the man that it would be very
difficult to do that since the phones were
all dead. The repairperson then suggested
that he contact the man via e-mail, but
since the company's Internet access was over
a phone line that didn't seem like a good
idea either.

YOUR BRAIN—DON'T LEAVE HOME WITHOUT IT

A woman had just purchased several items she needed from a department store and was handed the credit card receipt to sign. The cashier noticed that the back of the woman's credit card wasn't signed and told her she couldn't complete the transaction without a signed card. The woman was slightly confused by this request, but she complied and signed the back of the card immediately after signing the receipt. The cashier took both the receipt and the card, held them up, and compared the signatures. Surprisingly they matched.

RUN FOR THE BORDER

A young woman went to her local Taco Bell and told the person behind the counter that she wanted her tacos to have only "minimal lettuce." The employee apologized to the young woman and told her they didn't have minimal lettuce—they only had iceberg.

There isn't an Internet company in the world that's going to fail because of mistakes—Internet companies make thousands of mistakes every week.

—iVillage founder and CEO **CANDICE CARPENTER** (February 1998) shortly before the bottom fell out of the dot-com market

THEY THREW A PARTY BUT DIDN'T INVITE ME

Because of a recent wave of "downsizing," an unnamed printing company was holding a good-bye luncheon for one of their oldest and dearest coworkers. The lunch was great and everybody was having a wonderful time until the manager cheerfully said, "This is fun. We should do this more often." As expected the room fell silent.

Stupid Warning Labels

Found on children's cough medicine:
Do not drive car or operate machinery.

IT'S ALL THERE
IN BLACK AND WHITE

A light-skinned black woman sued her employer, a municipal agency located in Norfolk, Virginia, for racial discrimination. She claimed she was discriminated against because she was black stating she was born and raised black and brought up in the company of black relatives. Four years later, she filed a similar complaint against the same agency, this time charging racial discrimination against her because she looks white. Maybe she wasn't discriminated against because of the color of her skin but by the content of her character.

A PERFECT DREAM WORLD

In keeping with our politically-correct and diversity-driven society, Mattel came out with Share-a-Smile Becky as part of its Barbie collection. Although we're not sure what's wrong with her, Becky is confined to a wheelchair. Unfortunately, the company's marketing plan hit a snag when it came to light that Barbie's Dream House is not wheelchair accessible. It has doors that Becky's wheelchair can't navigate through and an elevator column that's perfect for Barbie but that Becky won't be able to use. A future Dream House design has corrected those problems. No word on whether Becky is suing for OSHA violations.

DRAWING THE CURTAINS

A woman called the Canon help desk about a problem with her printer. The tech, wanting to know what operating system she was using, asked the simple question, "Are you running it under Windows?" The woman paused and then said, "No, my desk is next to the door, but that's a good point. The man sitting in the cubicle next to me is under a window, and his is working fine." Makes you wonder what system she was operating under.

A harried passenger called his travel agent from the airport with an urgent question. "How do I know which plane to get on? The agent asked exactly what he meant, and the man replied, "I was told my flight number is 823, but none of these darn planes have numbers on them."

MOUSE IN THE HOUSE

Overheard in a computer shop:

Customer: Yeah, I need a mouse pad.

Salesperson: No problem, sir, we've got a large variety.

Customer: But will they be compatible with my computer?

THAT SCARED
THE CRAP OUT OF ME

An unidentified woman in Acton, Massachusetts, called police complaining that someone had stolen her bathroom. Even with such a weird claim, police still sent a patrol car over to check things out. When they arrived, they were shocked to discover the woman was telling the truth; her bathroom *was* gone. The sink, the toilet, the tub, and the walls had been torn out and all the debris had been removed. Police interviewed neighbors and discovered they had seen a van marked "Image Tile" parked outside the woman's house. Following up on their investigation, they learned that the company had sent the workers to the wrong house, and once they realized their mistake, they left. A spokesperson for the company said they would repair the woman's bathroom. No sh . . .

THEY SAID WHAT?

More "How did they get hired" statements taken from résumés and cover letters as printed in *Fortune* magazine (July 21, 1997). Here are some highlights:

1. "I demand a salary commiserate with my extensive experience."

2. "Received a plague for Salesperson of the Year."

3. "You will want me to be Head Honcho in no time."

4. "Marital status: single. Unmarried. Unengaged. Uninvolved. No commitments."

5. "Note: Please don't misconstrue my fourteen jobs as 'job-hopping.' I have never quit a job."

6. "Marital status: often; children: various."

7. "Reason for leaving last job: They insisted that all employees get to work by 8:45 A.M. every morning. I couldn't work under those conditions."

8. "Finished eighth in my class of ten."

A LOOSE CIRCUIT

The following are actual questions received by employees of an electronics store:

- "How much do you guys sell the illegal satellite receivers for?"

- "The phone is supposed to be cordless. Why does it come with a cord?"

- "How long do you soak alkaline batteries in water to recharge them? How many times can I do it?"

- "I just switched from dial-up to cable Internet. Is it the same Internet?"

NEWSPAPER AD:

Mixing bowl set designed to please a cook with round bottom for efficient beating.

BORDER PATROL

Here are more examples of companies reaching across our borders into Mexico to sell their products, but forgetting that sometimes things get lost in the translation.

 With the huge success of the campaign "Got Milk?" the Dairy Association expanded their advertising to Mexico. It was soon brought to their attention that the Spanish translation of "Got Milk?" became "Are you lactating?"

 Another Mexican mistake was the Coors slogan, "Turn it loose." In Spanish it became "Suffer from diarrhea."

 An American T-shirt maker in Miami printed shirts for the Spanish market that promoted the Pope's upcoming visit. Instead of, "I saw the Pope," (*el Papa*), the shirts read, "I saw the potato," (*la papa*).

GOING POSTAL

A janitor working the graveyard shift at a post office in Portland, Oregon, needed to get some supplies and went to the maintenance closet to retrieve them. When he opened the door, he surprised two supervisors, a man and a woman, half-clothed and in the middle of an intimate embrace. Immediately, the woman blurted out, "We were just looking for a lightbulb." Later, the janitor was called into the manager's office and told that if he said anything about the incident he would be fired. A little too late I'm afraid, as he had already revealed the details of the revealing situation to several people. The entire work unit was called to a special meeting later that day. The supervisor scolded his employees: "There's a rumor going around the office right now and anyone caught spreading any rumors will be fired." One employee, who at the time hadn't heard the "rumor," spoke up. "With all the rumors going around this office, how do we know which rumor is the one we're not supposed to spread unless you tell us what it is?" The supervisor glared at the worker and made a blanket statement: "Just don't talk about it." There are good and bad outcomes to this story. The good one is that no one was fired for spreading the story; the bad one, the male supervisor's wife heard the story and filed for a divorce. Since the man worked at the post office, I wonder if she sent him the divorce papers by certified mail.

I DON'T THINK THAT'S WHAT THEY MEANT

More from the "Lost in Translation" file:

 Scandinavian vacuum manufacturer Electrolux used the following in an American campaign: "Nothing sucks like an Electrolux."

 Clairol's curling iron, the "Mist Stick," hit the German market with a plop—the word "mist" is German slang for manure. A "Manure Stick" doesn't sound like something people would want to use to curl their hair.

 Colgate introduced a toothpaste in France called "Cue." Unfortunately, this is also the name of a notorious adult magazine.

 Frank Perdue's chicken slogan, "It takes a strong man to make a tender chicken" was translated into Spanish as "It takes an aroused man to make a chicken affectionate."

MOVING ON UP

For its film *Jefferson in Paris* about Thomas Jefferson's life in Paris serving as ambassador to France, the Disney Company took out a full-page newspaper ad promoting the movie. The ad depicted scenes from the movie, including one that showed Jefferson and part of the Constitution. No big deal, right? Well, as most high school students should know, Jefferson wasn't involved with writing the Constitution—he wrote the Declaration of Independence. When the error was pointed out, a spokeswoman for Disney said, "We all walked in Monday morning and said, 'Oh, fu**'" We hold these truths to be self-evident: Not all publicity companies are created equal.

I received a fax once with a handwritten note on the bottom to please fax the document back to the sender when I was finished with it, because he needed to keep it.

—Asked-to-remain-**UNNAMED OFFICE MANAGER**

MY FINE FEATHERED FRIEND

An animal sanctuary warden took home a beautiful blue and gold macaw parrot named Oliver for the night to give him special attention. While the bird was at her house, the woman started giving very special attention to her boyfriend and soon they were in the throws of a passionate night of sex. The next morning the woman took the bird back to the sanctuary and that's when it opened its big trap. "God—o— God," he squawked. "How do you like it?" he mimicked. The woman knew full well where the bird had learned those phrases, and so did everyone else in the room. "Oliver's attention to detail left nothing to the imagination. It sounded like he was reliving every moment from the night before," said the woman's boss. The macaw was kept away from visitors and everyone went out for a cigarette.

WHY DO YOU WANT TO WORK FOR THIS COMPANY, AGAIN?

During a job interview, the prospective employee was diligently answering the questions in a manner that would most impress the interviewer. Things were going along quite well when there was a knock at the door. Was it another person eager to get his interview underway? Nope, it was the pizza delivery guy. "He had arranged for a pizza to be delivered to my office," recalled the human resources executive. "I had to ask him not to eat it until later." Sound like a bizarre interview situation? Well, read on!

- There was a long pause after the interviewer asked a question. The reason for the delay became apparent when the applicant began to snore.

- When asked why the interviewee went to college, he answered, "To party and socialize."

- One potential employee claimed she had graduated cum laude but had no idea what cum laude meant. However, she said she was proud of her grade point average: It was 2.1.

COURTING TROUBLE

Jennifer Sutton, an executive assistant at a Fortune 500 computer company, was anxious to perform her civic duty and fulfill the summons to serve on a jury. She told her boss, Senior Vice-President of Finance Warren Edwards, several times that she would have to take time off during the trial. However, the night before she was to begin serving on the jury, Edwards gave her a late-breaking assignment. Sutton worked all night and even came in early the next morning to finish up, but Edwards demanded she stay. "I felt like I was going to be late and would get into trouble. I was in tears and told Mr. Edwards that I needed to go to jury duty," Sutton said. "He said for me to pack up my stuff and consider this my last day, that I was fired." In a move most employees can only dream of, District Judge John Marshall was so angered when he heard Sutton's story, he issued an arrest warrant for Edwards. County deputies went to his office, took him into custody, and brought him before the court. One can almost hear the cheering in the office once the boss hit the other side of the door. "I made it clear to him that this was not one of his smarter management decisions," said Judge Marshall. Most people try their best to get out of jury duty, but apparently when you have a boss like this, sitting on a hard wooden chair for weeks on end would seem like a vacation.

COLOR BLIND

A boss stormed into a worker's office and demanded to know why his orders hadn't been followed explicitly. He wanted the woman to use the company's Canon Laser Color copier to print a white object on a dark piece of paper. The boss didn't believe the worker when she claimed that that wasn't possible and accused the woman of just being lazy. Finally, the worker took the boss over to the printer, opened up one of the cabinets, and pulled out the toner cartridge. She showed her boss that there wasn't any "white" toner--only cyan, magenta, yellow, and black. The only thing that turned white in the room was the boss's face when all the blood drained out of it.

Customer: Can you copy the Internet for me on this diskette?

YOU'VE GOT THE POWER

A day after a lightning strike had destroyed the in-ground cables of a company's computer system, the repairs had been done, and the system was back online. The phone rang in the computer programmer's office, and the man answered the call. It was from the head of the company who said tersely: "In the future, please give me advance notice of any emergency so that the customer service department will have time to shut down their computers and make other arrangements to service customers." How do you know when bosses are going to say something stupid? Their mouth is moving.

YOU SEND ME

A technician received a frantic call from a customer claiming his computer's internal fax modem was faulty. After nearly an hour of back-and-forth questions and answers it turned out the man had been trying to fax a letter by holding it in front of the computer's monitor and pushing the Send key.

My computer doesn't power on. Also, I tried to call you on the cordless phone I bought there, and it isn't working either.

—Call received by an **ELECTRONICS STORE** during a widespread power outage.

SCREENING THE IGNORANT

One computer technician was given the job of keeping other employees up to date on the most current technology, and he did that by teaching computer classes to the company's staff. One day during basic computer class, he instructed the class to move the mouse to the upper left corner of the screen and click on the menu. One student raised his hand and complained that nothing was happening. The instructor came over and stood behind the man while he repeated the procedure. The cause of the problem became immediately apparent. The man had actually picked up his mouse, placed it on the monitor, and clicked. This guy was so computer ignorant he probably thought RAM was a dirty word.

A COMPUTER HACKER

A technical support assistant overheard a coworker speaking with a client on the phone. It was apparent that the man on the other end of the phone was having a problem getting his network card working. After several minutes of questions, the coworker put the phone on hold and started laughing hysterically. He turned to the tech support assistant and said, "I don't believe it. This guy's complaining that his network card isn't working. The idiot said the card was too long for his expansion slot—so he sawed off the end!"

OUT FOR LUNCH

Lightning was flashing and thunder was booming overhead as the graphics department and most of the sales department gathered around the large plate-glass window watching one of nature's most splendid shows. The manager of the newspaper made a request that the employees stay in the office until the storm passed. The receptionist for the company came bouncing into the office and said, "Well, how can you tell if it's stopped raining?" Even though the thunder was rocking the office you could still hear a pin drop.

BEAT THE CLOCK

A worker knocked on his boss's door and asked permission to go home early for the day. The boss asked if there was a problem, and the man replied that he was just very, very tired. The man looked exhausted and the boss was concerned that something else might be wrong. "Are you all right, Donald?" he asked. "Yeah, like I said, I'm just real tired," replied Donald. "Oh?" exclaimed his boss. "Yeah," said Donald. "Daylight Savings Time was last night, and I'm just beat after staying up until two in the morning to set my clocks back."

THE NUMBER YOU HAVE REACHED

Every month when the phone bill came in, the office manager from a textile company in Sacramento, California, knew
there was going to be trouble. And every month she was
right—the billing statement was incorrect. She tried and
tried to find a phone representative to help her with the
problem, and after several attempts found someone whom
she thought was capable and in a position to help. The
manager told the representative of the billing problem and,
as it wasn't something that could be handled over the
phone, was asked to come down to the phone company to
correct it. Finally, the woman thought, here is someone with
half a brain. Happy that she had found someone to relieve
her situation, the woman asked a simple question; "Where
are you located?" The representative quickly replied, "At my
desk." Seems like the office manager was right—the phone
representative did have half a brain.

THE HAND THAT FEEDS YOU

A man who relies on a Labrador retriever as his Seeing Eye dog was told by a federal agency that helps administer the Americans with Disabilities Act that he could no longer bring the dog to work because one of his coworkers suffers from a fear of dogs. Another case of the blind leading the blind.

Here's a tip from page sixteen of the *Hewlett Packard Environmental, Health & Safety Handbook for Employees:* Blink your eyelids periodically to lubricate your eyes.

KEYLESS ENTRY

A man who worked for the state in Hawaii was sent to jail on his fourth criminal conviction, but he didn't lose his job. While serving time on weekends, he continued to work five days a week at his regular job as a prison guard. Isn't there a saying about a fox watching the henhouse?

THE JOYS OF DEALING WITH THE PUBLIC

Customer (inquiring about a VCR that had just returned from being serviced): So, what the hell was wrong with this thing anyway?

Electronic Repair Shop Worker (reading service receipt): It says here they removed a foreign body that was lodged in it.

Customer (angrily grabbing the receipt): Well, now I know you're lying. That VCR has never been out of the United States, so how the hell did it get a foreign body stuck in it?

Phone call from an elderly woman to a pharmacy: "Can you call my doctor and see if there is another medication he can prescribe for me? The metal foil on those suppositories really hurts!"

Lowe's Hardware Worker: How can I help you?

Customer: Yeah, umm, do you have a McDonald's in here?

Lowe's Hardware Worker: No, sir, this is a Lowe's Hardware Center.

Customer: So that means no McDonald's, huh?

WHAT'S IT WORTH TO YA?

The Association of Community Organizations for Reform Now (ACORN), an activist group that fought for legislation to increase the minimum wage to $5.75 an hour, filed a lawsuit in California to exempt itself from paying its employees the current minimum wage of $4.24 an hour. In their legal brief, the group argued for exemption on the grounds that "the more that ACORN must pay each individual outreach worker, the fewer outreach workers it will be able to hire." Looks like the ACORN doesn't fall too far from the tree.

WAKE ME WHEN IT'S OVER

A memo from the Personnel Appeals Board of the State of New Hampshire:

> Ms. Dobe, an employee of the Labor Department, is appealing a written warning issued to her for sleeping at her desk. Ms. Dobe alleged that she had not been given sufficient time since her first warning to correct her problem of sleeping at work. She also alleges that the Department of Labor had an obligation to be more proactive in assisting her with overcoming her "sleeping problem."

You know, if a warning didn't make her wake up and take notice, I don't know what will.

THE DUES AND DON'TS

The Taylor Crop Newsletter reported that a grievance had been filed against Mills College, an eight hundred-student women's institution, by Teamsters Local 70 in Oakland, California, citing a violation of an agreement with the union. The Teamsters claimed the school contracted nonunion workers to clear about forty acres of poison-ivy-infested land, and they demanded restitution. The union stipulated that the school be forced to award back pay for the members who lost out on the work or, as an alternative, that the five hundred nonunion workers who cleared the field be forced to join Local 70. The five hundred nonunion individuals in question were unable to answer these charges since they are--goats. Seriously, the five hundred goats that cleared the land were hired from a company called "Goats R Us." I'm still not sure what the union was thinking; I mean, where is a goat going to keep his union card anyway?

AN UNREASONABLE FACSIMILE

One of the job requirements for a woman working in the accounts payable department of a certain company was to make sure employee expense reports were filed properly. Company policy mandated that every reimbursement request had to be accompanied with a receipt. One day, she received an expense report without a receipt and immediately called the man who had submitted the claim. The man told her that he couldn't find the receipt but that he had paid for it with his credit card. The accountant asked if the man would please fax over the credit card statement that showed the purchase, and she would be able to cut him a reimbursement check based on that proof. Within the hour, a coworker entered the woman's office with a fax and a look of disbelief on her face. Instead of his credit card statement, the man had faxed over a copy of his actual credit card, showing his account number for the whole world to see. Let's just hope the man's doctor never asks him to fax over a copy of his last prostate exam.

THIS COMPANY GOT FLOCKED

An Aramark employee at the company's Oak Brook, Illinois, office tried to enter his building but was blocked by two angry Canadians—geese, that is. He went to another door, but a third goose hurried over and blocked his way. "It started acting crazy," said the fifty-seven-year-old man. "I tried to hurry in the building, but it flew at my face. It was very ferocious." As the frightened man turned to run, he fell and broke his wrist. Aramark refused to pay his workers' compensation claim for the injury, so the man sued. Unfortunately, his attorney couldn't find any similar cases to serve as precedents for the employees claim, and he argued that the building "was a 'high-goose' area, as opposed to a high-crime area." It's not clear whether Aramark's attorneys bought the argument or whether they didn't want to run the risk of getting really goosed in court, but they settled with the man for $17,767.54. So it looks like Aramark got the goose and got the bill.

A DOUGHNUT SHY OF A DOZEN

In a cliché come to life, several people witnessed a police helicopter land in a vacant lot next to a Krispy Kreme doughnut shop in Albuquerque, New Mexico, at 1 A.M. According to a department spokesman, "The contracted pilot and a police officer landed the copter early in the morning, ran in and grabbed a dozen, came back out, and took off." The spokesman went on to say, "We've been given no reasonable excuse as to why they would even think they could do this." The officer and the pilot are under investigation and face possible charges of misuse of city funds—probably because they didn't bring enough to share.

When he tried to unload one tank into another already full tank, a worker at the Brown-Forman Distillery accidentally sent 1,800 gallons of tequila into the sewer system.

ARRIVE ALIVE

When people think of stressful jobs they might think of a heart surgeon, the President of the United States, or even a member of a bomb squad. But one driving instructor learned the hard way that she might win the award for the most stressful job—at least in this case. A teenage student and her driving instructor were casually pulling into the parking lot of the DMV testing center after successfully completing her driving test, but instead of putting the car into park, the teen stepped on the accelerator and plowed into four parked cars. Then the vehicle spun out of control and hit two more cars. A pedestrian walking nearby was pinned between two cars as one struck by the teen careened into another one. The driving instructor was treated for shock and stress in the hospital and was sent home to recover. The young girl was also taken to the hospital with minor injuries. She received a failing mark after the multivehicle crash, although initially she had passed.

THIS CUSTOMER WAS ALREADY FRIED

Drive-Thru Customer: How many pieces of chicken are in that ten-piece box?

Mrs. Winner's (Chicken) Employee: (pause) There are . . . ten . . . pieces of chicken . . . in the ten-piece box.

Drive-Thru Customer: Well, is there any white meat in that?

Mrs. Winner's Employee: A ten-piece is normally one breast, two ribs, two wings, two thighs, and three legs. It's half and half.

Drive-Thru Customer: Well, how many pieces are there in the fifteen-piece box?

BIG MAC ATTACK

In order to keep the general public from becoming confused about who's who, companies are allowed to trademark their names so other companies can't use them. One of the most diligent protectors of their name identification is McDonald's. They've gone after mom-and-pop companies, medium-size companies, and even companies owned by people named McDonald—and won. But McDonald's suffered a setback in the UK when London's High Court allowed Frank Yu Kwan Yuen's registration for "McChina" as a British trademark for his restaurant. "It appears to me on analysis that McDonald's are virtually seeking to monopolize all names and words with the prefix Mc or Mac," Judge David Neuberger ruled, and that there was an "absence of any evidence of confusion" among the general population from the Chinese restaurant's name. After hearing the court's ruling, Yuen said he was "as happy as a drunken prawn." An item, I hope, that doesn't appear on McChina's menu.

LELAND GREGORY

DO NOT PASS GO—
DO NOT COLLECT $200

The police see all kinds of idiots while
doing their jobs, and usually they get to
arrest them, too. Case in point: A janitor
who saw a man hiding in the Randolph County
Courthouse in Muncie, Indiana, after hours
called police. The man stayed around long
enough for officers to arrive on the scene,
and they chased him for about a block. The
twenty-six-year-old man obviously had no
sense of direction because he ran right to
the door of the county jail. He was arrested
and charged with burglary, theft, criminal
mischief, resisting arrest, and public
intoxication. "We love it when they run to
the jail for us," said sheriff's spokesman
Ken Hendrickson. The man went from resisting
arrest to insisting on arrest.

HALF AS OLD AS MOSES' TOES . . .

Some idiots steal for fun and the thrill, some because they can't help themselves, some for no reason at all, and some out of necessity. At a Wal-Mart store in San Diego, California, a man was confronted by a security guard for allegedly stealing six packages of Dr. Scholl's corn remover. The two men got into a short scuffle, and the thief got away—but not very far. According to a police spokesman, "The suspect was unable to run away because of the corns on his feet." The police never made fun of the man's corns because that would have been too callous.

Nike announced to great fanfare that it was raising the minimum wage for its Indonesian workers. They would now get the equivalent of about $37 per month—which in the United States would barely buy one half of one Air Jordan shoe.

A COLD RECEPTION

The two mental health workers in London, England, who paid a home visit to a woman suffering from paranoid schizophrenia got annoyed because the woman refused to speak to them. In fact, she sat with her back to them and never answered any of their questions or acknowledged their presence; "She didn't seem to want us there," said one health worker. The following day, two other health workers paid a follow-up visit to the woman and immediately found out why she had given the other two a cold shoulder—she was dead.

A SHOT IN THE DARK

After their shift had ended, two police officers in Peru were in the station locker room changing clothes when a stroke of bad luck happened. One of the officers checked to see if his revolver was loaded and accidentally shot his partner in the genitals. The man rushed to his wounded partner's side and administered first aid until help arrived. Even though it was an accident, the police officer's gun was seized and checked for defects, while the officer himself was placed on administrative leave pending an investigation into the shooting. A friend of the police officer said, "He is absolutely distraught. It was a million-to-one accident that ended up with a man losing his penis." I've heard of someone going off half-cocked before, but this is ridiculous.

CUSTOMERS SAY
THE DARNDEST THINGS

 An employee at a retail store saw a customer struggling with an armful of items. Trying to be helpful, he asked if the patron wanted a shopping basket. Her reply was, "Don't you think I've got enough to carry already!"

A pharmacy employee in Pennsylvania received the following question: "When the prescription says *zero* refills, does that mean I can't get it anymore?"

Cellular Phone Representative: Yes, all of our plans have nationwide free long distance.

Customer: So I can call all of the thirty-six states?

An employee at a doughnut shop dealt with the following exchange:

Customer: How much are the jam doughnuts?

Doughnut Employee: They're $1.60 each.

Customer: Well, how many can I get for a dollar?

GETTING A HANDLE ON THE SITUATION

We've all gotten tired of our coworkers at one time or another and have secretly dreamed of different forms of revenge. But masturbating into his colleagues' coffee cups? That's what one Syracuse, New York, social services employee is accused of doing. The man was caught red-handed, and his victims, experiencing a range of emotions, have been offered counseling and medical tests. The man was arrested and has been charged with three counts of second-degree harassment, three counts of criminal nuisance, and three counts of public lewdness. Looks like he really took matters into his own hands.

Stupid Warning Labels

Found on a can of windshield deicing spray:
Spray works in subzero temperatures.

HO, HO, HO

Christmas is the busiest time of the year for the post office. People mail millions of boxes, cards, and letters to friends and relatives everywhere in the world. It's a happy time, a joyous time. So it came as some surprise to the good people of Ohio when twelve thousand pieces of mail carried an unusual greeting of holiday cheer. Instead of a brightly stamped MERRY CHRISTMAS, the Yuletide mail recipients got a Scroogy YOU BITCH printed on their mail, courtesy of their local post office. It gives the expression "Ho, ho, ho" a whole new meaning.

INDENTURED SERVANT

A female employee and her supervisor went out to a local bar in Otautau, New Zealand, to have drinks after work. During the course of the evening, the supervisor suddenly dropped to his knees. Was he proposing? Nope, he tried to bite the buttocks of the woman but was unsuccessful because his false teeth fell out before he could get within biting range. The woman filed a sexual harassment complaint for $4,175 (U.S. dollars) but was turned down by an Employment Tribunal. They made their decision based on inconsistencies in the woman's story and the fact that the alleged harassment happened away from the job. We've all had a supervisor who was a pain in the butt, but this guy got carried away.

IT'S ONE OF THOSE NEW-FANGLED THINGS

A call to an Internet provider elicited the following conversation:

Customer: So this modem will get me connected to the Internet, right?

Tech Support: Yes, sir. That will do it.

Customer: And that's the latest version of the Internet, right?

Note on a job application: "Please call me after five-thirty because I am self-employed and my employer does not know I am looking for another job."

TAKE TIME OFF TO TAKE TIME OFF

British workers were urged to bum around, stop working, and in effect, do nothing in order to celebrate the second annual National Slacker Day, but the event wasn't as popular as you would expect. A poll conducted during that week showed that 59 percent of the people claimed they don't do much at work anyway. Instead, they use company time to talk with friends and family and catch up on correspondence through the company e-mail. The special day of observance to celebrate doing nothing generated hardly any interest—people slacked off doing anything to celebrate National Slacker Day—making the event, at the same time, both a success and a failure.

LELAND GREGORY

INCONVENIENCE STORE

The manager of the Hawkeye Pantry store in Des Moines, Iowa, opened early for business and found a man sleeping inside on the floor. After the man rubbed the sleep from his eyes, he explained to the manager that he had accidentally gotten locked in the store when it closed the night before. As he couldn't get out, he decided to pass the time guzzling down a few beers from the cooler. The man seemed apologetic and offered to pay for the beers. After the manager rang up the purchase, the man left the store. About twenty minutes later the manager noticed that more than just beer was missing. In fact, at least $3,500 in cash and a roll of lottery tickets were gone. "It just didn't click that he was paying me with my own money," the manager said. "It was early. I wasn't thinking." Hum, a manager who wasn't thinking—sound familiar?

NO JOKING MATTER

A lot of actors take out insurance policies to protect them from fanatical fans, accidents, and loss of whatever they're known for (nice legs, pug nose, etc.) But one group of actors decided to take out an insurance policy in case they got sued. The organization Clowns International recommended that its members take out "custard pie insurance" in case they were sued for hurting someone when they toss a pie. A spokesclown for the organization said that because of "an increasingly litigation-crazy public," not to mention "the ethics and legal implications of 'splatting' and 'sloshing,'" that its members should be protected. Clown Bluey said: "Clowning is a serious business. If I was a businessman in my best suit I wouldn't appreciate someone coming over and throwing a load of gunge at me." Bonzo the (Almost) Famous Clown, from East London, said: "If you do throw something at a person, they have every right to throw it back. It's all quite harmless really." Martin "Zippo" Burton, honorary vice president of Clowns International from Southampton, England, admitted that to date no clown has been sued, but since a lot of people can't take a joke, it's only a matter of time before the courts see a case named "John Q. Public versus Slappy the Clown."

SHE'S GOT A LOTTO NERVE

A twenty-eight-year-old employee in a Fenton, Missouri, convenience store found a $100,000 winning scratch-off lottery ticket, but she won't be able to collect. An investigation alleged the woman stole the ticket from her place of business. In fact, she is accused of stealing nearly thirty tickets a day in the hopes of getting a winner. The woman's activities came to light when a coworker turned her in. Did the woman see the ticket thief doing wrong and feel compelled to alert the police in order to get her back on the straight and narrow? Nope, the accused woman had promised her coworker $2,000 to keep quiet, and when she refused to pay up, the "stool pigeon" went to the police. After getting busted for the scratch-off lottery scam, I bet the woman scratched her coworker off her Christmas list.

SIGN, SIGN, EVERYWHERE A SIGN

A twelve-year-old girl at Stony Brook School in Branchburg, New Jersey, learned sign language after her hearing was damaged because a student set off some fireworks in the hallway. But now it's the young girl who's in trouble. Apparently the principal at her school threatened to suspend her for "doing sign language after being told it wasn't allowed on the bus." Westerholm later confirmed that "sign language, or any behavior, is not permitted if it is going to cause a disturbance on the bus," but he never communicated how signing could "cause a disturbance." How is it that the people with the least amount of common sense are the ones making most of the decisions?

A BIG FLOP

Most people have been party to horseplay at work, but one employee at a meat-packing plant in Beccles, in Eastern England, obviously got carried away. Three men held down a 140-pound employee as a coworker nicknamed "Honey Monster," who happens to weigh 320 pounds, performed a belly flop on the restrained man. The resulting prank left the victim with several cracked ribs. A judge ordered "Honey Monster" to perform 180 hours of community service and paid the injured man $1,000. Compared to this prank, getting popped with a rubber band isn't so bad.

A restaurant in Hong Kong was ordered to shut down by authorities after it came to light that they were using old underwear as dishcloths.

CUSTOMERS, CUSTOMERS EVERYWHERE AND NOT A BRAIN IN SIGHT

A customer e-mailed his cell phone company seeking help for a problem: "My phone is lost somewhere in my house, the battery is dead, and the phone is set on vibrate. What can I do to make it ring so I can find it?"

Pizza Hut Employee: Pizza Hut, sorry we're closed.

Customer: How late are you open tonight?

A manager at a large bookstore chain was helping a customer find the history section that was located upstairs. Once the two got to the top of the stairs, the manager pointed out the location of the books the woman had requested. The woman smiled and said, "So, are these books, like, to buy?"

TWICE CHARMED

When Frank Biondi, Jr., was fired as chief executive of Universal Studios, he received a severance package worth $30 million, which was on top of the $15 million severance package he received in 1995 when he was fired as chief executive of Viacom.

Stupid Warning Labels

A different brand of insect spray: kills flies, wasps, mosquitoes, midges, and other flying insects. Not tested on animals.

BREAK LIKE THE WIND

A Scotland Yard spokesman confirmed that the Department of Professional Standards was investigating a complaint about one of their officers. The owners of a home that was raided during a drug bust filed the complaint. The homeowners felt the officer's actions were "rude and unprofessional," and they demanded an apology. What did the officer do? He was accused of passing gas in the owner's hallway and then not apologizing for the offending odor. Who knows, maybe it was just a new form of tear gas.

AN EMERGENCY SITUATION

A Houston ambulance driver, who obviously thought he was a police officer, made an unscheduled stop at a doughnut shop while en route to the hospital. Not the most idiotic coworker story unless you realize that the ambulance driver still had a patient in the back of his vehicle. This, combined with several other incidents (like transporting former Mayor Bob Lanier to the hospital in an unlicensed vehicle), prompted the Texas Health Department to begin an official investigation into the Houston Fire Department.

I'LL KEEP AN EYE OUT FOR YOU

A sexual harassment lawsuit was settled by a Safeway store in Kapolei, Hawaii, when a male employee was caught spying on a female customer through a restroom peephole. He was caught when the woman realized she was being watched and shoved a toilet plunger handle through the hole and into his eye socket. Apparently the man wasn't lying when he said he got a real eyeful.

Note on a résumé: "I was proud to win the Gregg Typting Award."

EXPIRATION DATE

A businessman called his travel agent and wanted to get all the pertinent information for a trip to China. The agent went over the protocol of getting his passport and shot records, but when he brought up the fact that the man would have to have a visa he was interrupted. "I've been to China before, sir, and I know for a fact that I don't have to have a visa." The agent logged onto his computer and pulled up the requirements for a visit to China, sure enough, a visa was needed. He got back on the phone and told the business-man that the agent had checked the requirements—a visa was necessary. The man shot back, "I'm sorry, pal, but you're wrong. The last time I went to China, they accepted my American Express."

THAT'S JUST GOOFY!

After two months of negotiation, the management of Walt Disney World finally relented and no longer makes the costume character actors share their underwear. Before the final settlement, the actors were allowed to wear only Disney-provided underwear, which was laundered and passed out randomly. An actor complained to management that the underwear was often not clean, smelled bad, had stains, and "things have been passed around." Actors will now be allowed to have personal underwear, which Disney will issue, and the employees can take it home and launder it themselves. Of course, this won't affect the character of Donald Duck because, as we know, he doesn't wear any pants.

YOU WON'T BELIEVE WHAT I HEARD

Municipal workers in the city of Cascavel, Brazil, have been banned from gossiping in the office, and breaking the ordinance is punishable by reprimand, mandatory sensitivity training, and dismissal. The law was passed in order to protect senior government workers whose reputations could be damaged by rumor and innuendo. In this case, the truth won't necessarily set you free, but it could get you fired.

WOMAN FINED FOR NOT GIVING 30-DAY NOTICE BEFORE DYING

—Fitchburg [Massachusetts] Sentinel and Enterprise headline

A RADIANT EMPLOYEE

It's an unfortunate occurrence in a lot of businesses: employee theft. People steal all types of things including pens, pencils, paper clips, even a tube of plutonium. Yep, a tube of plutonium. A forty-seven-year-old employee of a decommissioned nuclear fuel reprocessing facility in Karlsruhe, Germany, is under investigation after he "borrowed" a tube of plutonium and took it home. The incident came to light when a routine screening found the man to be highly contaminated, apparently because he not only stole the tube, he also must have opened it to look inside. The man's girlfriend and daughter were also contaminated as was his house and car. The man probably got a "glowing" recommendation—of stupidity.

HAVE A NICE DAY

An unidentified man entered a Home Depot in
Oklahoma City, grabbed an ax, and used it
as a weapon to rob the store. He then left
with the money and the ax and proceeded to
run the same routine at two other stores,
including a Wal-Mart. Witnesses at the
Wal-Mart reported that when the man entered
the store the greeter, wanting to do his
job properly, smiled at the man and placed
a sticker on the ax so when he left he
wouldn't be charged for it.

BENT OUT OF SHAPE

During a meeting of the Lincoln, Rhode Island, School Committee scheduled to discuss the possible hiring of two assistant principals, one female member reached over, grabbed the nose of a female colleague, and began twisting it saying, "What's the matter? Did you get your little nose twisted out of joint?" Other members of the committee said the tension between the two women had been building for a while. The proposition ended with three I's and two Nose.

WHAT'S IT WORTH TO YOU?

The only way this bank teller would have noticed that the currency in front of her was phony is if the counterfeiter had printed on it, "This is fake money!" It seems a woman opened an account at the First National Bank of Newport (Pennsylvania) using a $1 million bill. Obviously the bank teller didn't know much about money because the largest bill value in circulation now is $100—the bill she casually accepted was worth ten thousand times that much. The teller happily opened a new account for the woman (no word if she gave her a free toaster or what). The counterfeiter was finally caught when she withdrew some of the money from her newly opened account and transferred it to her husband's account. The woman was arrested and held on $25,000 bond. I hope the bondsman didn't accept a $25,000 bill.

DON'T GET YOUR NOSE OUT OF JOINT

The police department in Northumbria, England, agreed to pay "several thousand dollars," as workers' compensation, to a detective who now suffers from chronic snoring. The detective, who originally asked for $25,000, claimed that the years he spent in the evidence room inhaling dust from seized marijuana plants caused him to have a whistling in his nose and severe snoring, which caused marital dishar-mony. It also caused a fifteen-year contact high.

A man looking for a job went
to his local Employment Service
at lunchtime only to see a
sign on the door saying,
CLOSED DUE TO STAFF SHORTAGE.

TAKE A LOAD OFF

In an article from the Associated Press, La-Z-Boy recliner tester Tim Nelson said the job of sitting down, propping up his feet, and rocking back and forth in the company's chairs all day is much harder than it looks. "It's not like they give us popcorn and a TV set to watch," complained the tester. "[Up] and down all day [can] be a workout," he said. To back up his seemingly ridiculous complaint the man's colleagues admit the job isn't that easy because testers must certify the comfort and balance of up to 130 recliners a day (10 to 15 pieces per day do not pass the rigorous tests). I wonder what kind of chairs they have in the break room?

SAY WHAT?

More from the "Lost in Translation" file:

 It was not until sometime after General Motors introduced the Nova in Latin America that it found out that No-va means, "It won't go."

Jolly Green Giant translated into Arabic means "Intimidating Green Ogre."

 In Chinese, the Kentucky Fried Chicken slogan "Finger-lickin' good" came out as "Eat your fingers off."

Hunt-Wesson introduced its Big John products in French Canada as Gros Jos before finding out that the phrase, in slang, means "big breasts."

WE'RE LOOKING FOR A FEW GOOD MEN

A top job recruitment firm in England suddenly received a staggering fifty thousand hits to their Web site in just thirty-six hours. Every request was an inquiry about the firm's latest posting by an unnamed company. The company's advertisement offered £45,000 a year to "fun-loving people" for three days' work per week—as actors in pornographic films. It was noted in the qualifications that applicants needed to have "an inquiring sexual mind." The ad even piqued the interest of some actual porno actors—160 to be exact. A spokesman for the employment Web site said: "Although our one adult model vacancy has been removed, we still have 43,000 sexy jobs in accountancy." I suppose accountancy can be a sexy job—I mean how many people have been screwed by their accountants already?

INSERT TAB "A" INTO SLOT "B"

A customer relations person at an e-commerce help desk was trying in vain to get credit-card information from a customer. The man on the other end of the phone insisted they should be able to read the credit card information and that something was obviously wrong with their equipment. The customer relations person couldn't understand what the man was talking about or how he thought they already had his credit-card information. After several minutes it became obvious that the man had stuck his credit card into the floppy disc drive of his computer thinking it would somehow send the information to the e-commerce help desk.

QUICKLY GETTING THE POINT

We've all heard the old, gruesome expression "putting your nose to the grindstone," but a warehouse worker from Oldham, England, took things one step farther. The unlucky employee stood up quickly, not realizing there was a six-inch nail sticking though a piece of wood above him. The man was literally nailed to a fifteen-foot plank and couldn't move until the fire department came. Strangely enough the nail did not pierce the forty-four-year-old's skull, and he fully recovered from his work-related accident. I'm sure the jokes about hitting the nail on the head got old very fast.

THE COLOR OF MONEY

Citing the Americans with Disabilities Act, a former traffic-light installer is suing Palm Beach County seeking lost wages dating back to his firing in 1997. So why did the county let the traffic-light installer go? Because the man was color blind and couldn't distinguish between the red and green wires or any of the other nineteen differently colored wires in a traffic light. So when the man first got his pink slip, I wonder what he thought it was?

A travel agent received a call from a man who asked, "Is it possible to see England from Canada?" The agent replied that it wasn't, and the man said, "But they look so close on the map."

LETTER OF RECOMMENDATION

A newly hired receptionist at a law firm was given the assignment of writing a letter to a client, but the task seemed to tax her capabilities.

Receptionist: In a letter, what goes after "dear"?

Office Manager: Whoever you're writing the letter to. You know, "dear somebody."

Later on when the office manager picked up the letter from the receptionist's out-box, she noted that it began, "Dear Somebody." Well, you get what you ask for.

AND NOW A WORD FROM OUR SPONSOR

The former chairman and CEO of AOL/Time Warner's Turner Broadcasting division has laid down the law and argued that viewers have a moral obligation to watch television commercials. Jamie Kellner said, "Your contract with the network when you get the show is you're going to watch the spots." "Otherwise," he said, "you couldn't get the show on an ad-supported basis." He claims people who use VCRs to record the shows and then later watch them and skip past the commercials are particularly irresponsible. The CEO vehemently stated that by not watching the commercials, "You're actually stealing the programming." But what about the age-old habit of getting something to eat or going to the bathroom during the commercial breaks—is that permitted according to our "contract"? Only if you really have to go, he answers, there's only "a certain amount of tolerance for going to the bathroom." Talking about going to the bathroom is perfect as it relates to this guy because he's obviously full of sh*t!

THERE'S WOOD IN
MORE THAN THEIR SHOES

Holland's National Archive and census office computer in
Maastricht came to a crashing halt when a thirty-two-year-old
civil servant overloaded the computer. The twenty-year-old computer system wasn't prepared to handle as much downloading
as the man had requested, and things went a little haywire.
National Archive director Philip Maarschalkerweerd said the
incident came to light when "one of our employees said his
computer had frozen and called the help desk. The systems
manager saw porn pictures appearing on the screen. He immediately realized what had happened. We don't collect information
of that kind." The National Archive's employee had overburdened
the ancient computer system with a huge download of porn.
The employee, who was not publicly identified, faces disciplinary
action. It's a wonder he doesn't sue for workers' compensation
for carpal tunnel syndrome in his wrist—for using the mouse,
you dirty-minded person.

SAME AS IT EVER WAS

A customer service representative received an e-mail from a client the company had worked with before. The person the client was used to dealing with had left the company, and a new employee had filled the position. This was obviously more than the client could handle. He said the following to the Customer Service Rep:

Client: John Martin used to be the manager for this store. Now you're telling me that Jill Halpern is the new manager?

Customer Service Rep: Yes, sir, that's correct.

Client: But the e-mail address you've just given me—manager@companyname.com—is the same as the old manager's e-mail address.

Customer Service Rep: Yes, sir, that's right.

Client: So if I send an e-mail to this address which one is going to get it?

CRAZY HIRING PRACTICES

Disgruntled postal workers turning violent have become such commonplace occurrences that even the worst stand-up comedians use such events in their acts. But the Equal Employment Opportunity Commission created the ultimate "punch" line in hiring practices. An article in the *Employee Relations Law Journal* explains, "Many individuals who become violent toward customers or coworkers suffer from some form of mental disorder. Yet for an employer to be too careful in screening potentially dangerous persons out of the workforce is to invite liability for discrimination under the ADA [Americans with Disabilities Act], while to be not careful enough is to invite tragedy and horrendous liability for negligent hire or negligent retention." Damned if you do, damned if you don't—and damned if it isn't just going to get worse.

TALES FROM A TRAVEL AGENT

- A woman in Little Rock, Arkansas, called a travel agent and said, "I want to book a flight to Pepsi-Cola on one of those computer planes." The agent thought for a moment and then responded: "Do you mean you want to fly to Pensacola on a commuter plane?" Without hesitating the woman replied, "Yeah, whatever."

- A man who had booked a vacation in Orlando, Florida, called his travel agency and voiced a complaint. He lambasted the agent because he had expected his hotel room to have an ocean view. The agent was at a loss as to how the man could expect a view of the ocean, since Orlando is located in the middle of the state. The man wasn't buying the agent's explanation and screamed, "Don't lie to me. I looked on the map and Florida is a very thin state."

TECH STOCK POP

"Unlike with other famous bubbles . . . the Internet bubble is riding on rock-solid fundamentals, perhaps stronger than any the market has seen before. Underlying the crazy price increases are the foundations of what could become the early 21st century's leading growth company. Just because the Internet stock phenomenon looks like a bubble, it isn't a given that the bubble will burst." From a column in *News.com* by CIBC Oppenheimer analyst Henry Blodget, January 1999—shortly before the dot-com debacle.

NEWSPAPER AD:

And now, the superstore—unequaled in size, unmatched in variety, unrivaled inconvenience.

JUST SAY NO!

A firefighter in Springfield, Massachusetts, who was charged with possession of crack cocaine and Oxycontin was fired from his job. Makes sense, right? Well, he wasn't fired for possessing the drugs, he was fired because he was caught smoking a cigarette when the state trooper arrested him. Smoking, either on the job or off, is a violation of state law for any firefighter or police officer hired since 1988. I suppose that while he's serving time in jail he'll have time to catch up on his smoking habit. As for his crack problem, that might take on a whole new meaning.

TOO BAD THEY DIDN'T PAD THEIR RÉSUMÉ

More "How did they get hired?" statements taken from résumés and cover letters as printed in *Fortune* Magazine (July 21, 1997). Here are some highlights:

1. "I procrastinate, especially when the task is unpleasant."

2. "Personal interests: donating blood. Fourteen gallons so far."

3. "As indicated, I have over five years of analyzing investments."

4. "Am a perfectionist and rarely if if ever forget details."

5. "I was working for my mom until she decided to move."

6. "I am loyal to my employer at all costs. Please feel free to respond to my résumé on my office voice mail."

7. "I have become completely paranoid, trusting completely no one and absolutely nothing."

8. "Reason for leaving last job: maturity leave."

9. "Failed bar exam with relatively high grades."

HATS OFF!

Tokyo's famous bullet train, which can hit speeds of 167 mph, was noticed creeping along at between 13 to 18 mph. It turned out that the train had been placed on autopilot and for at least five minutes, the controls were unattended. What was the problem? The driver, who is required by the Central Japan Railway to always wear his hat, had "left the driver's seat to look for his hat after he realized he wasn't wearing it," a spokesman said. We know the company has a policy on wearing hats, but what about leaving the controls? Actually, there wasn't a rule against doing that until after that event; "We have notified all drivers that they should continue driving until they reach a station, after which they should report that they have misplaced his or her hat." If they hire employees this stupid, I hope they have rules regarding not leaving your brain at home.

GET ON THE RIGHT TRACK

A loaded passenger train on one of England's busiest routes was delayed for more than an hour because of a technical problem. Some passengers left the train and found alternate ways to their destinations; others waited it out. Everyone was fairly calm as delays can happen at anytime, but when they found out the reason for the layover they were flabbergasted. It seems the driver was lost and didn't know the way to the next stop. The man actually backed the train up to the previous station to ask directions. "He sounded very flustered and muttered that our driver needed to ask another driver the way," recalled one of the passengers. "We could not believe what we were hearing. A huge groan came over the carriage. Some of the lights were not working, and the buffet bar was closed." At least the conductor had one thing going for him—he still had on his hat.

IT'S CRIME TIME

The city commission of Chiefland, Florida, was forced to put the city's seven police officers on indefinite leave after they realized there was a little problem with the city's charter--it didn't give police authority to make arrests or issue citations. The charter only gave police authority to enforce city codes and ordinances. At one time, the officers had general police powers under a state statute, but for some reason that statute was repealed years ago. Oh, I can see the lawyers lining up with their convicted clients now, can't you?

A menu at a local diner in Cotton Plant, Arkansas, had the following item:
BLT—$1.75 with bacon—$2.25.

TOO BAD YOU'RE NOT ALLOWED TO KILL THEM

 Customer Service: Do you have your account or customer number?

Customer: No.

Customer Service: Do you have the model and serial number of your machine?

Customer: No, but I have the account number. Will that help you?

Movie Theater Worker: Hi, what can I do you for today?

Lady: Yes, um, how long do your matinees run until?

Movie Theater Worker: Six P.M. every day of the week.

Lady: Oh. So is the 2:55 P.M. show still considered a matinee?

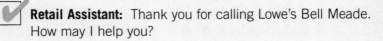 **Retail Assistant:** Thank you for calling Lowe's Bell Meade. How may I help you?

Customer: Yeah, is this the Lowe's store in Bell Meade?

Retail Assistant: Yes, sir, it is. How may I help you?

Customer: Oh, just checking to see if this was the number for the one in Bell Meade.

LICK ME

In a fit of civic pride, the Howick Village in New Zealand decided to produce its own postage stamps. More than twenty thousand stamps were printed especially for the village, but somewhere down the line there was a slight error. Was it like the famous "Inverted Jenny," the twenty-four-cent stamp with the biplane printed upside down? Close, but the problem with this stamp was that on the back there wasn't any glue, and on the front there was. That's right, the printer accidentally printed the entire run with the glue on the front. The town has since received a new batch of stamps, and it's a good thing they stopped with the stamps—no telling what would have happened with the envelopes.

THE ULTIMATE COMB-OVER

The Edinstwo 35 company in Panicino, Bulgaria, was forced to file bankruptcy and liquidate its remaining assets in order to pay creditors. Unfortunately, they also had 630 employees to whom they owed back pay and only one thing left over from the bankruptcy to pay them with--combs. Each employee was given hundreds of colored combs in lieu of back pay. Some workers said they would now try and sell the combs (worth approximately 30 cents each), while others boasted: "I can throw a comb away every time I comb my hair. I've got enough for the rest of my life." At least the former workers will be well groomed while they stand in line at the unemployment office.

WHAT WOULD DR. ZAIUS DO?

Most people have had a lousy job at one time in their career—you might be having yours now. But a group of zookeepers in Dudley, England, could claim one of the smelliest jobs around when a local supermarket donated an enormous batch of Brussels sprouts to the zoo and the orangutans developed a taste for them. The zoo is considering issuing gas masks to its keepers because; "Orangutans are windy animals, and because of all the Brussels sprouts they are eating, there is quite a pong around here at the moment," according to monkey keeper James Harper. He added: "Whoever gets the short straw gets to muck them out." So tell me why, when we were kids, our parents wanted us to eat Brussels sprouts?

HER WORK LEFT A LASTING IMPRESSION

The State Department awarded a $15,000 bonus in recognition of "outstanding performance" to the head of the office that permitted thirteen of the September 11 hijackers to enter the country via expedited U.S. visas. The woman was asked to step down from her position after it came to light that the "Visa Express" program, which allowed Saudi nationals to obtain visas over the Internet without ever being seen by a U.S. official, was responsible for allowing so many of the terrorists to enter the United States. Richard Boucher, State Department spokesman, unabashedly made this statement about the bonus: "The performance of people is examined very carefully by committees, and they determine who gets the pay benefits," he said. "People get these performance awards based on things that they've done and how they've performed in their jobs and met the needs of the service. It's a sign that they performed well in terms of serving their country and their government." But which country and whose government?

A FOOL FOR A CLIENT

A lawyer acting in his own defense challenged his bribery conviction at a Florida Court of Appeals hearing and lost. He then turned around and filed a petition to have the conviction reversed. The court asked on what grounds his request was based. He responded that as his lawyer, he had failed to inform himself adequately that acting as his own lawyer was a bad idea. He lost that one, too.

British ice cream manufacturer Wall's has announced it will no longer print jokes on its ice cream sticks because too many customers don't "get" them.

WHY A DUCT?

The owner of a Massachusetts day care center and several of her employees were sued by the parents of a child in their care. The parents found out that the owner, obviously intrigued by the versatility of duct tape, wanted to find out if it really did "work on everything"--and taped their child to the wall. The child was not physically harmed and feels relieved to have survived a very sticky situation.

FLY ME TO THE MOON . . .

A woman called her local travel agency requesting information to plan a trip to Cape Town. The agent started giving her all the information on the length of the flight, price, and passport information. When he got to the part about passports, she stopped him. "I'm not trying to make you look stupid," the woman said, "but Cape Town is in Massachusetts." By his very trade, the travel agent is extremely familiar with the locations of cities and countries, and he said, "I'm sorry, but Cape Cod is in Massachusetts, Cape Town is in South Africa." The woman quickly responded by slamming down her phone.

FROZEN ASSETS

The owner of a metals analysis business was on a business trip and got drunk. There's nothing too special about that. But while stumbling around in a stupor he broke a window to gain entry to a company-owned trailer in order to get inside and out of the subzero temperatures. Unfortunately, he left the outside door open after he passed out on the floor, and when he woke up, the fingers and thumbs on both hands were so frostbitten they had to be amputated. The Wisconsin Supreme Court ruled that because he was on a business trip, the man was entitled to workers' compensation. I'll drink to that.

A STAND-UP GUY

An employee at a Birmingham, Alabama, publishing firm stayed behind his desk for five days straight without sleeping, eating, or even moving because, as it turned out, he was dead. The owners of the company are wondering why not one of the other twenty-three employees in the open-plan office noticed their coworker had been figuratively a working stiff. The man's condition was finally revealed when a janitor asked him why he was still there during the weekend—and got the cold shoulder.

Steve Hilbert was fired from insurance giant Conseco after decreasing the company's market capitalization by billions. What did the company do to him for running the company into the ground? They gave him $75 million in severance pay— beats the hell out of a gold watch.

FOR THE LOVE OF . . .

Tech Support: All right, sir. If you could double-click on the Applications Icon.

Customer: That's why I hate Windows. Icon. Look, I'm a Protestant, and I don't believe in icons.

Tech Support: Well, that's just an industry term, sir. I don't believe it was meant to—

Customer: I don't care about any "industry terms." I don't believe in icons.

Tech Support: Well, why don't you click on the "little picture" with a big A on it.

Customer: That's more like it.

THE MAIL'S NOT THE ONLY THING THAT'S CERTIFIED

"Going postal" has become part of our lexicon—meaning, of course, someone who becomes violent (named because of the high number of postal employees who lose it on the job). One clerk at Denver's downtown terminal annex was escorted from the building after he "exhibited some bizarre behavior besides wearing a dress." Although the clerk was informed he should go home and stay away from the annex, he returned twice that day wearing not only the dress but also a gorilla mask and something authorities described as a strap-on sexual device. The police were called to the scene, where they discovered several guns and two hunting knives in the man's pickup truck. Surprisingly, a psychiatric evaluation was ordered.

AND YOU LOOK LIKE A BUCKET OF . . .

A Dutch construction site supervisor was arrested in Ghana, West Africa, after he was caught using his fellow workers' water bucket as a toilet. The man admitted to the transgression but claimed he was suffering from diarrhea, and there was no Port-A-Potty on the site. Police weren't convinced of the man's sincerity and charged him with causing a public nuisance. And you thought your boss was tough.

According to a survey conducted in London, England, bosses think more than one in ten of their employees are incompetent at their jobs.

TAKING A LOAD OFF AT WORK

A case that went all the way to the U.S. Supreme Court involved a man who had filed a lawsuit under the Americans with Disabilities Act. He claimed he was fired from his job as a forklift operator despite his federally protected disability of sexual dysfunction. The forklift operator asserted he usually engaged in sexual activity five or more times a week, but that an injury limited him to twice a month—and after that, he said, his place of business no longer viewed him as a good worker and downsized his position. I guess that's not the only thing that got downsized.

TAKING A SLICE OUT OF CRIME

The manager of a pizza restaurant in Lakewood, Ohio, was arrested and eventually indicted for stealing $38,000 from the company—not just in dough, mind you, but also in dough. In an effort to bolster her store's sales figures, the woman fabricated big call-in orders and then took the pizzas home. Not only did her ploy work in sales figures, she also became part of the company's upper crust and had her picture in the company newsletter. She eventually got busted, however, when she asked the pizzeria's owner to help her move to a new house and he discovered more than four hundred rotting, moldy pizzas stacked to the ceiling in a spare room. It's very possible the woman was arrested in thirty minutes or less.

GETTING A HEAD IN BUSINESS

According to a "Work-Love Balance" survey
conducted in London, England, nearly two
thirds of employees said they had "enjoyed
physical intimacy" in their workplace, with
favorite places being the elevator and the
stairwell. The results of the 1,072-worker
survey showed that the nasty nurse and
dirty doctor stereotype was false because
medical workers are the least likely to
indulge in workplace romances. So who is
most at risk for "working overtime"?--
employees in the leisure and tourism indus-
tries, where eight out of ten have "pulled
an all-nighter."

RECYCLE, REUSE, AND RIDICULOUS

Recycling is a noble endeavor, and I give kudos to the people who work at recycling organizations, businesses, and plants for their dedication and tolerance relative to the stupid calls they get. Here is a sampling of some of the idiotic phone calls received at the Portland, Oregon, metro recycling information hotline:

- "Where can I recycle six hundred dresses, several dozen bottles of Jim Beam, a thirty-year-old box of Howdy Dowdy ice cream cones, and a few dozen wigs?"

- "How can I recycle a couch soaked with blood?"

- "How do I dispose of 'household' dynamite?"

- "Do you have a safe pesticide for the bug burrowing a hole in my husband's arm?"

- "What should I do with a hundred breast implants that have been removed and preserved in formaldehyde?"

BETTER LATE THAN NEVER

A fifty-two-year-old man in Calcutta, India, who had applied for a state government job finally got the interview he was hoping for—thirty-four years later. Ravindra Nath Halder was just a teenager when he applied at a state labor exchange office in West Bengal. More than three decades later, Ravindra, now a grandfather, was very surprised to get the letter saying an interview had been granted for the position. Mohammad Amim, India's Labor minister, said it often took "a long time" for a person to be called for an interview. No word on whether the man got the job or not. If this is typical of the Indian government, I hope the man has already applied for retirement benefits.

DRINKING ON THE JOB

A Frenchman went out with his colleagues during a business trip to Russia and wound up dying from alcohol poisoning after he drank too much vodka. The man's wife went to court after her social security fund refused to pay her the pension she would have received if her husband had died on the job. A French court ruled his death a "workplace accident" because his business required him to attend the party. Leave it to the French to endorse drink till you drop as a job requirement.

At a museum in London, a brass plate with Braille writing for the blind reads:
PLEASE DO NOT TOUCH THIS EXHIBIT

A REAL SECRET SAUCE

In order to ensure that diners return to his newly opened eatery, a Beijing restaurant owner was discovered putting in a very special ingredient. The restaurant, which had done a booming business since it opened, served a specially prepared spicy fish dish that included a little kick—ground opium poppy. The owner said he would appeal the arrest, and thousands of strung-out customers await his release.

WORKING YOUR WAY UP FROM THE BOTTOM

A "whistle-blower" is someone who discovers and then reports illegal or unscrupulous activity in the workplace. One vigilant British worker, who obviously had some spare time on his hands or intestinal problems, measured several rolls of toilet paper and found they only had 200 sheets as opposed to the 320 sheets stated in the contract with the supplier. His employer, West Somerset District Council, demanded the vendor wipe the slate clean and was awarded $28,100. The employee's compensation for saving the company nearly $30,000? He was given a few days off. So if the company is ever "rolled," you can be sure who did it.

A DREAM DESK

Right after lunch, we all get a little sleepy and dream of taking a quick nap like we did in kindergarten. German engineer Matthias Knigge has taken the concept of siesta and put a modern spin on it. He designed a desk that converts into a giant pillow for office workers who fall prey to post-lunch lethargy. The prototype of the desk, made in walnut, looks normal in every way until a small hidden button is depressed. A panel in the desk opens up as a fan inflates a bright orange airbag that, I suppose, will keep hunters from shooting you while in slumber. No word on when the desk might hit America because the development team keeps trying out the product.

According to a recent survey,
Britons spend more than ninety
minutes a day gossiping, e-mailing
friends, and flirting in the office.

THE BEST SEAT IN THE HOUSE

A patron at a Stockholm, Sweden, restaurant walked into the men's room and noticed all the toilet seats were missing. As he was talking to the manager, the man looked into the kitchen and saw an employee emptying the dishwasher with the missing toilet seats among the dishes. The manager tried to convince the customer the freshly washed toilet seats would be warm and pleasant to sit on. The customer told him to "sit on this" and called the health inspector.

PAGING OLIVER NORTH

In order to give the appearance of keeping current and having all their files in order, two Immigration and Naturalization Service supervisors in Laguna Niguel, California, allegedly ordered their subordinates to shred approximately ninety thousand documents that were backlogged in their office. They also, again allegedly, instructed the workers to continue shredding any incoming documents until the office was current. This was less than two years after the attacks of 9/11. Maybe that's why the initials for the Immigration and Naturalization Service are INS—there are fewer outs and more INS.

RALPH KRAMDEN ROLLED OVER IN HIS GRAVE

Either he was unclear of the concept, couldn't read, or was just overzealous in his job, but a parking warden in Manchester, England, gave a ticket for parking at a bus stop to a bus driver who had stopped to pick up passengers at a space marked "Buses Only." "All my passengers queuing to get on were gobsmacked when the warden dashed over," remembered the bus driver. "He said the area was restricted. When I asked restricted to who [sic], he replied, 'Buses.' I thought he must be blind." After a complaint to the local council, the warden was required to be "retrained." Maybe the man was dyslexic and he thought the bus was at a sub stop.

THERE'S NO SUCH THING AS A DUMB QUESTION—OR IS THERE?

The following are actual questions received by the Portland, Oregon, metro recycling information hotline:

- "Can someone from the government come out to my house and smell my living room?"

- "Where can I get a permit to burn my house down?"

- "How can I dispose of five semi trucks full of inedible marshmallows?"

- "What happens when you cut a worm in half?"

- "How can I recycle guinea pig droppings?"

- "What do I do with a ten-year-old pile of manure?"

FROM THE COLONEL TO THE KLINK

In what might possibly be the biggest idiots-at-work story, a nineteen-year-old in Philadelphia was arrested and convicted of robbing a Kentucky Fried Chicken store. Nothing terribly odd about that, until you realize it's the same KFC the man had worked at for two years. Also, when he robbed the store he wore no mask or disguise, and all the employees recognized him. In addition, since he had worked at the store for the past two years, he should have remembered that the store's safe is time-locked at 9 P.M., but he started his robbery at 9:15 P.M. and therefore got no money. Amazingly the man was able to hide from police for three days, and even more amazingly, on the third day he showed up for work as if nothing had happened. One thing did happen, however; the manager called the police, and the man was arrested.

WHO PUT THE CUSS IN CUSTOMER?

Domino's Pizza Employee: Thanks for choosing Domino's. Will this be carryout or delivery?

Customer: Do you guys deliver?

Lowe's Employee: You have to pay up at the front desk, sir.

Customer: Where's the front?

Lowe's Employee: (baffled) Uh . . . at the front.

Customer: Well, every store is different.

A motion picture theater manager stopped a man from bringing a bag of food into the movie citing company policy prohibiting outside food. The man got irate and started screaming at the manager. "Look," he bellowed. "I can't eat a lot of junk, so how can you deny me entry with food that is healthy enough for me to eat?" It was obvious from the smell and the familiar golden arches on the bag that the man was not trying to smuggle in health food.

Why are all of your Christmas CDs not out like they are in December?

—Overheard at the music section of Wal-Mart around Easter

DON'T BE A NAME CALLER

When British authorities decided to merge the University of Bradford and Bradford College, they paid a consulting firm $30,000 to come up with three choices for a new school name. What names did this highly paid, professional consulting firm come up with? Bradford University, University of Bradford, or The University of Bradford. The chairman of Bradford Council's education scrutiny committee had this to say of the consultant's job: "It is farcical. A six-year-old would have been able to deliver the same judgment with ease. The money could have been better spent." If a six-year-old could have done it why didn't the University of Bradford or Bradford University professors come up with the name instead?

Sign outside a furniture
store in northern Virginia:
ANTIQUE TABLES MADE HERE DAILY.

A REAL TRAVEL ADVENTURE

A rather confused woman told her travel agent, "I want to go from Chicago to Hippopotamus, New York." Needless to say, the agent was rather confused by the request. "Are you sure that's the name of the town?" "Yes, I'm sure," said the client. "What flights do you have?" The agent got on the computer and tried every airport code in the country but couldn't come up with a city named Hippopotamus. She finally got back on the phone and told the client that she had had no luck locating a city with that name. "Oh, don't be silly. Everyone knows where it is. Check your map!" The agent scoured the map of New York State looking for any city that might vaguely sound or look like Hippopotamus. Finally, as a last-ditch effort, she asked the woman, "You don't, by any chance, mean Buffalo, do you?" "Oh, right, that's it. I knew it was a big animal."

HEAD CLEANER

Anyone who works in a retail store has to deal with stupid customers asking stupid questions, and the video rental business is no exception. Even when signs are clearly posted and straightforward the customer whose mind is on rewind still asks the zinger. Here are some actual questions asked of video rental employees:

- "Do you have any movies?"

- "It's due back by ten A.M. in the *morning?*"

- "How come it's not out on video yet?" (The answer: It had just opened in the theaters.)

- "I'm looking for an action movie, but it can't have any swearing, sex, violence, or questionable language. What do you recommend?"

ONE DOWN AND TWO YARDS TO GO

A woman who was looking for a bolt of cloth approached an employee of Wal-Mart who worked in the Crafts/Fabrics department. The woman said she had a project that required thirty yards of fabric but had a question:

"How long is thirty yards?" she asked.

"In feet?" asked the Wal-Mart employee, trying to clarify what the woman was asking.

"No, in yards," the woman shot back.

"How long is thirty yards in yards?" the employee questioned.

"Yes, don't you understand English?" the frustrated woman complained.

"Yes, ma'am, I do," the employee calmly stated. "Thirty yards is thirty yards."

"Are you trying to be smart with me!" the woman bellowed.

"No, ma'am. . . . . I tell you what," the Wal-Mart worker said. "Why don't we get a yardstick and figure out how much thirty yards in yards would be."

"That's more like it," the woman retorted.

Thirty yards is thirty yards but this woman really put her foot in her mouth.

FORGIVE THEM FOR THEY KNOW NOT WHAT THEY DO

Although volunteers aren't exactly employees, there was one group that was so asinine I had to include them in this book. The overzealous volunteers at a British church in Newquay, England, were running a rummage sale ("Jumble Sale" to the Brits) to help raise money. In order to get as much stuff as possible to sell off at bargain prices, one of the volunteers accidentally snatched the church's gold and silver objects (valued at $15,000) added them to a box with some not so expensive bric-a-brac, and sold the entire collection of valuables for about $15! May the Lord be with them.

Was met with a string of broken promises and lies, as well as cockroaches.

—Response to a question on a job application,
"Why did you leave your previous position?"

LET'S SEE WHAT DEVELOPS

A female customer inquiring about color film approached a woman in the camera department of a local retail store. The clerk asked the woman what size film she was looking for, and the woman held up her hands about eight inches apart. "It's about this big," she said. "It's black with a brown knob on top." The clerk took a deep breath because she knew she had a live wire on her hands. She slowly explained to the woman that there are many different sizes of film and she needed to know the number in order to make sure customers got the proper one. The woman became very indignant and spoke loudly enough so that others in the store could hear her: "That's the trouble with this store— nobody knows anything about the products they sell!" And she stormed off without her film and without a clue.

MORE THAN JUST
THE COMPUTER CRASHED!

A worker complained to his computer support department. He argued that the limit of one computer at a time being allowed access to their emergency dial-up connection shouldn't pertain to him because, he said, referring to his iBook, "This one isn't a computer—it's a laptop!"

MANAGEMENT NEEDS REWIRING

A manager called his technical support department demanding to know why the network was suddenly down. It took several minutes until a technician finally figured out that the manager had unplugged a router so he could charge his cell phone. A lot of companies have gone wireless but this guy was clueless.

Physical disabilities include minor allergies to house cats and Mongolian sheep.

—From an actual job application

WHY DID THE CHICKEN CROSS THE ROAD?

KFC Employee: Welcome to KFC drive-thru, this is Ken—can I take your order?

Drive-Thru Customer: Let me get a McChicken.

KFC Employee: (pause) I'm sorry, a what?

Drive-Thru Customer: A McChicken sandwich.

KFC Employee: Um . . . McDonald's is next door, this is KFC.

Drive-Thru Customer: Oh! Well, do you have a chicken sandwich?

KFC Employee: (pause) Yes, we do. Which chicken sandwich would you like? The Classic, the Big Crunch, the Spicy Big Crunch, or the Twister?

Drive-Thru Customer: I want the McChicken—you know! The McChicken???

WHAT'S FOR DINNER?

In what has got to be one of the stupidest excuses in the world, a restaurant owner in Australia claimed that a moldy bowl of chicken pieces, chicken stock, tomatoes, chilies, salad dressing, and limes and a bowl of chutney infested with fly larvae found by the health inspectors were not meant to be sold but were for his own personal consumption. And in one of the stupidest judgments in the world, the Melbourne magistrate who heard the case believed him and dismissed twelve of the charges brought against the owner by the Health Department. I hope the judge didn't accept the offer of a free dinner at the man's restaurant. Actually, I hope he did.

Instrumental in ruining entire operation for a Midwest chain operation.

—Unfortunate misspelling on a job application

DON'T DO AS I SAY, DO AS I MEAN

A supervisor for a janitorial crew instructed a newly hired janitor to pick up all the trash in the building and throw it in the Dumpster. Later, when the supervisor went through the building inspecting the crew's work, he noticed all of the trash baskets were missing. He instinctively went out to the Dumpster, and there he found all of the trash baskets piled up in the Dumpster. The man had literally done what he was told to do—he picked up all the trash in the building and threw it in the Dumpster.

ODD JOBS

Express Personnel Services based in Oklahoma City compiles the Annual Odd Jobs Survey. Here are some samples from the list of strange and unusual jobs:

- Santa Rosa, California: A person to ride along in a Federal Express delivery truck so the driver can use the car pool lane. $11/hour

- Someone to sit in a room with trial lawyers and listen to a dry run of the objections, closing arguments, and line of questioning they plan to use in court that day. $10.50/hour

- A person whose sole responsibility it is to work with a lawn care company to keep the kinks out of hoses. $6/hour

OUTDATED INVOICE

An account executive for a computer-consulting company was going through outstanding invoices and found a client who was delinquent in payment. In order to straighten out the matter quickly, the executive put together an invoice and e-mailed it to the client for payment. A few moments later, a reply to the e-mail was in the executive's inbox, and he was pleased at the speedy response. When he opened the e-mail, he was surprised to read that the company, based in Europe, agreed that they did owe the money, but company policy didn't allow invoices by e-mail. The letter informed the account executive that in order to receive payment in full, he would have to send a hard copy of the invoice to the same person by Federal Express. The executive thought it was strange that in this day and age a company couldn't simply print the invoice from the e-mail document and pay it. What made the executive more con-fused was the fact that the company that couldn't accept an invoice by mail was—Microsoft-Europe!

CURBSIDE SERVICE

While parked on a city street in broad daylight, and in front of pedestrians, two sanitation workers in Rochester, New York, were spotted utilizing the services of a prostitute in their city-owned trash truck, while on duty. Well, I guess she was on duty, too. Both men have families, and both men were fired. Said Mayor William A. Johnson, Jr., "This was probably the most expensive sex act that they've ever committed." More than likely their marriages are now trashed, too.

A technical support person working at a local ISP received the following call—Customer: "Hi, is this the Internet?"

BIG BROTHER IS WATCHING

The mayor of Cranston, Rhode Island, was criticized by the American Civil Liberties Union after it came to light that he had hired a private detective to make videos of city employees sleeping on the job. Coming to his own defense, the mayor said, "That's a public building, and there's not a reasonable expectation of privacy there." In response to the ACLU involving itself in his city, he also stated, "There is no civil liberty to sleep on the job." Well, the Constitution does make reference to "life, liberty, and the pursuit of happiness," and a good nap is a source of happiness to a lot of people.

YOU'VE GOT TO BE KIDDING ME!!!

This story might describe the most outrageous workers' compensation lawsuit on the books. The mother of a man who killed three coworkers and then turned the gun on himself is suing the company he worked at claiming that since he died on the job, he is eligible for workers' compensation. The company says it has no intention of settling with the woman.

ASLEEP ON THE JOB

Tech Support: If the computer goes to sleep just hit any key to wake it up.

Customer: Uh, I can't find it.

Tech Support: Can't find what, sir?

Customer: The "any key." Where is it?

Tech Support: It's just any key, sir. Just hit any key.

Customer: I'm telling you I can't find the "any key"! Don't you understand English?

In the "What Were They Thinking?" category: John B. McCoy was paid $10.3 million plus $3 million per year, when he retired from Bank One after laying off 5,100 employees.

FLUSHED WITH EMBARRASSMENT

The toilet-roll holders were replaced in all the bathroom stalls at a video production house. The holder was changed from the standard-size roll to the larger industrial roll enclosed in plastic casing. The janitor who replaced the holders walked into a meeting to explain that the holder, now of a different size, would require the occupants of the toilet to sit at a different angle. He went on to pontificate that since the rolls were also of a different size, it would now be necessary to pull the paper out in a different way. The janitor was surprised and shocked when the employees told him to "roll" out of there and leave them alone.

More "What Were They Thinking?":
Douglas Ivester was paid $17.8 million plus $3 million per year, on his retirement from Coca-Cola just after laying off 6,000 employees.

PHYSICIAN, HEAL THYSELF

The Rouse Company, a developer and landlord of a shopping mall, acknowledged that it had somehow forgotten to renew the lease on its own headquarters in Columbia, Maryland. The mistake, they admit, will probably cost the company somewhere in the neighborhood of $11 million. Now that the company moved into the neighborhood of $11 million guess whose rent is about to go up?

AIR KISS

To show their appreciation for a job well done, Air Canada gave each of its hundred best-performing customer service personnel a coupon (worth U.S. $3.75) redeemable only at restaurants owned by its in-flight food service contractor. Giving an employee a coupon for airline food--isn't that more like a punishment than a gift?

NEWSPAPER AD:

Get rid of aunts: Zap does the job in 24 hours.

IS THE CUSTOMER ALWAYS RIGHT?

Petsmart Employee: Thank you for calling Petsmart, how may I help you?

Customer: Can you transfer me to your pet department?

Receptionist: Springfield Mazda, how may I direct your call?

Customer: I need the automotive department.

Receptionist: Which one—Sales, Parts, or Service?

Customer: Where they work on cars, idiot.

Poster Mailing Employee: Thank you for calling Poster Mailing Services, how may I help you?

Customer: Cabinetry, please.

Poster Mailing Employee: This is Poster *Mailing Services,* as I said—not Lowe's. (The phone number was one digit off.)

Customer: Oh, so do you sell cabinets?

Customer: (poking her head in the door) Sir, are you open?

Employee: Yes, we are, ma'am.

Customer: So, I can come in and buy what I want?

A SERIOUS PAPER TRAIL

If the saying, "A clean desk is the sign of a cluttered mind" is true, then one eighty-five-year-old Philadelphia timber yard owner must have the cleanest mind in the world. Ray Kostin, owner of Rittenhouse Lumber, has two desks in his office that have approximately eighty cubic feet of paper on them. Kostin claims he hasn't seen the surface of his desks for forty-three years. He laughingly remarked that men in his community bring their wives to his office to show them he's messier than they are. In his own defense, Kostin said that he would like to clean up his desks, "but the customers keep interfering."

Stupid Warning Labels

**Found on a can of self-defense pepper spray:
Pepper spray may irritate your eyes. You also should avoid accidental contact with your eyes or mucous membranes.**

WHAT STARTS WITH AN "F" AND ENDS WITH A "CK"? FIRETRUCK

The fire chief of Braintree, Massachusetts, ordered a new $650,000 fire truck to replace the east side station's 1966 model. He knew the ladder truck wouldn't fit in the existing fire station, but he ordered it anyway. The chief then took sick leave, and no one followed up on renovating the firehouse. Now the new fire truck has to be kept at the main fire station 1.6 miles away and will be sent to the east side when needed. "In the best of times, this form of government doesn't have the best communication," said a town spokesman. Town financial officials leaped to the rescue and stated that they might be able to find the necessary money to fund a study on how to expand the station. The short answer on how to expand the station—make it bigger.

OPEN UP A SIX-PACK OF TROUBLE

"The change is not related to our drinking
habits but to our unique corporate culture
and working conditions," a Seoul, Korea,
Labor Ministry spokesman said. What he was
referring to was a newly instituted insurance
regulation whereby employees' injuries caused
by work-related drinking can be treated as
"industrial accidents," and employees therefore collect workers' compensation. I guess
they can now file a claim for carpel tunnel
syndrome from bending the elbow too much.

LELAND GREGORY

TAKING A LITTLE OFF THE TOP

An employee of an Athens, Georgia, animal vaccine manufacturer pleaded guilty to embezzling more than $1 million
from the company. The woman skimmed off the money
during the five years she handled the company's accounts
payable. According to authorities, she and her husband
spent some of the $1 million building an addition onto their
doublewide trailer. What kind of addition to a doublewide
trailer could one spend that kind of money on—an additional
four-bedroom brick house, maybe?

CITY WORKERS RARELY FIRED FOR DOING A BAD JOB

—*Houston Chronicle* headline

IT PAYS TO ADVERTISE

A guard at an armored car company pulled into the company parking lot in a new $53,000 Chevrolet Corvette. Officials for Dunbar Armored in Cinnaminson, New Jersey, approached the man and asked about the new car. Were they admiring his new wheels? Nope, they were curious if the guard's purchase of a new car had anything to do with the theft of more than $400,000, just days before. The guard admitted to the theft and was arrested. Maybe it would have been less conspicuous if he had built an addition to his Buick.

RUN AND GUN

A former tree cutter for the city of Moncton, Canada, showed up at work intoxicated, carrying a loaded sawed-off shotgun, and searching for his boss. It wouldn't be going out on a limb to guess that the man was immediately fired, but now his union is trying to help him get his job back. However crazy this may sound, even if the union is successful in reinstating the man, it will have to wait until he finishes his two-year sentence on weapons charges. I wonder whether Jimmy Hoffa is really dead or if he's just hiding out of embarrassment?

GIVING YOUR BOSS A DIRTY LOOK

A German man claims he was treated unfairly, and his physiological addiction wasn't taken into consideration before he was terminated. The former civil servant said his employers failed to take into account his addiction to pornography, and he shouldn't have been dismissed even though he ran up a $10,000 bill surfing porn Web sites at work. The company must have thought he was just seriously dedicated for spending so much overtime at work.

Would you like to ride your own ass?

—The Thai to English translated advertisement for donkey rides in Thailand

A DIFFERENT KIND OF LETTUCE

A woman in Weston, Florida, placed her order at the drive-thru menu board at McDonald's, and then drove forward to collect her food. The McDonald's employee handed her the bag through the window, and the woman drove off. No one can resist grabbing that first hot fry so when the woman stuck her hand in the bag, she was surprised to pull out a twenty-dollar bill. She was even more surprised when she looked in the bag and saw hundreds and hundreds of dollars. Knowing this wasn't a misplaced toy from a Happy Meal, the woman turned the car around and drove back to the restaurant. It turned out the bag she had been given contained the restaurant's entire receipts for the day. McDonald's officials promised to send the honest woman a thank-you letter and $50 in gift certificates. They were probably afraid to give the woman a cash reward because she might use the money at a real restaurant.

A MODEL WORKER

A man lost his job at the Delhi Department of Horticulture, and he sued for unlawful dismissal. He was granted his job back and paid back wages, fifteen years' worth, for his time off work. But when he was reinstated, the man was given nothing to do, although he still received a salary. Most people in his situation would love to have a completely stress-free job, but this man felt insulted. "People need to be able to feel that they earn their salaries," he says. "My misfortune is that I can't because I have been forced to remain idle. It's as if one has been paid to cheat." So he sued again, but this time he demanded to be given work to do while on the job. The court ordered the department to give the man something to do and has begun an inquiry into the waste of government funds. Searching out government waste will certainly give someone a lot to do for a long, long time.

WITHOUT THEM, WHO COULD WE MAKE FUN OF?

 Veterinarian Assistant: McDorman Animal Clinic, may I help you?

Customer: Yeah, there's a field of bluebonnets near my house and I'm worried that my dog might catch the blue-bonnet plague.

 Waiter: Can I get you anything to drink?

Customer: Ketchup!

Waiter: Would you like ice with that?

 Wendy's Employee: Can I take your order?

Customer: Yeah, on the grilled chicken sandwich, is the chicken grilled or fried?

 Bookstore Employee: It sounds like you're looking for an atlas.

Customer: I don't want an atlas, I want a book of maps.

THIS MAN IS ALREADY
PARTIALLY REFUNDED

A customer service representative received a phone call from a customer concerned about an item on *his* latest bill. "What's this DE 'bited'?" the man asked. The representative was confused and wasn't sure what the customer was referring to. The representative pulled up the man's account on her computer, which gave her an exact replica of the bill. The representative then asked the man if he could use the word in a sentence. He said, "This amount will be de-bited from your account on April 10, 2004." The representative had to put the man on hold so he couldn't hear her laughing. He obviously didn't know the meaning or the proper pronunciation of the word debited, as in this amount will be debited from your account. Obviously, there was something debited from his brain.

𝕿his is to inform you that a memo will be issued today regarding the subject mentioned above.

—**MICROSOFT**, Legal Affairs Division

LELAND GREGORY

AROUND THE WORLD
IN SEVEN MINUTES

A very pleasant-sounding woman called an
airline asking how it was possible that the
flight from Detroit left at 8:20 A.M. and
got into Chicago at 8:33 A.M. The ticketing
agent tried to explain to the woman that
Michigan was an hour ahead of Illinois, but
that just seemed to confuse her even more.
After giving up on explaining the concept
of time zones, the agent finally said, "The
plane goes very, very fast." The woman was
satisfied with this answer and hung up.

THIS GUY'S WIRES GOT CROSSED

An insurance agency whose company covers cellular phones and mobile equipment received a call one day from a man seeking a claim because his phone stopped working when it got wet. The agent questioned the man as to how the phone got so wet that the electronics stopped working, but the man procrastinated and wouldn't give her a satisfactory answer. Finally she asked, "Did it go into a pool, the ocean, or a lake?" The man took a deep breath and admitted his child had thrown the phone into the pool, but before the agent could say another word, the man blurted out that he didn't feel he should have to pay a deductible for the claim. The agent asked, "Why?" The man puffed up and said since the instructions didn't specify "Do not drop in water," he didn't feel like he was responsible for the damage. Please hang up and try again!

REBOOT YOUR BUTT

Young Customer: Yeah, hi. Uh, my computer crashed!

Tech Support: It crashed?

Young Customer: Yeah, it won't let me play my game.

Tech Support: All right, hit Control-Alt-Delete to reboot.

Young Customer: No, it didn't crash—it crashed.

Tech Support: Huh?

Young Customer: I crashed my game. That's what I said before. I crashed my spaceship and now it won't work anymore.

Tech Support: Click on "File," then "New Game."

Young Customer: (pause) Awesome! How'd you learn how to do that?